THE TERRY LECTURES

A COMMON FAITH

*Santayara :
Reason Religion
in Religion*

OTHER VOLUMES IN THE TERRY LECTURES SERIES
AVAILABLE FROM YALE UNIVERSITY PRESS

A
COMMON
FAITH

Second Edition

JOHN DEWEY

INTRODUCTION BY
THOMAS M. ALEXANDER

Yale UNIVERSITY PRESS
New Haven & London

THE DWIGHT HARRINGTON TERRY FOUNDATION LECTURES
ON RELIGION IN THE LIGHT OF SCIENCE AND PHILOSOPHY

The deed of gift declares that "the object of this foundation is not the promotion of scientific investigation and discovery, but rather the assimilation and interpretation of that which has been or shall be hereafter discovered, and its application to human welfare, especially by the building of the truths of science and philosophy into the structure of a broadened and purified religion. The founder believes that such a religion will greatly stimulate intelligent effort for the improvement of human conditions and the advancement of the race in strength and excellence of character. To this end it is desired that a series of lectures be given by men eminent in their respective departments, on ethics, the history of civilization and religion, biblical research, all sciences and branches of knowledge which have an important bearing on the subject, all the great laws of nature, especially of evolution . . . also such interpretations of literature and sociology as are in accord with the spirit of this foundation, to the end that the Christian spirit may be nurtured in the fullest light of the world's knowledge and that mankind may be helped to attain its highest possible welfare and happiness upon this earth." The present work constitutes the latest volume published on this foundation.

CONTENTS

INTRODUCTION

THOMAS M. ALEXANDER

In December 1994, three young explorers in the Ardèche region of southern France noticed a draft of cold air issuing from behind a pile of rocks. Discovering a narrow opening, the woman in the group, Eliette Brunel-Deschamps, slipped through the narrow tunnel until it opened onto a ledge overlooking a vast chamber. When she returned with her companions and a portable ladder, they descended to the floor and began to realize that the walls were covered with images of Ice Age animals—wooly rhinoceroses, mammoths, bison, lions, and horses—as well as painted silhouettes of hands and abstract designs. Deep inside, a cave bear skull had been ceremonially placed on a low rock, its canines just protruding over the edge. Thirty thousand years ago, the cave had been a shrine for shamanic rituals connecting the human hunters with the spirits of the animals whom they hunted and with whom they coexisted. "Alone in that vastness, lit by the feeble beams of our lamps, we were seized by a strange feeling. Everything was so beautiful, so fresh, almost too much so. Time was abolished, as if the tens of thousands of years that separated us from the producers of these paintings no longer existed. It seemed as if they had just created these masterpieces. Suddenly we felt like intruders. Deeply impressed, we were weighed down by the feeling that we were not alone; the artists' souls and spirits surrounded us. We thought we could feel their presence; we were disturbing them."[1]

The discovery of Chauvet Cave (as it is now known), and of other caves filled with prehistoric art, gives us an insight into the emergence of human consciousness, into the time when we became human. The hunters of Chauvet lived in a religious world rich with symbols, reverence, awe, and ceremony. And we can understand the reaction of the explorers, which is not just aesthetic admiration or scientific curiosity. They, too, felt a sense of awe mingled with the presence of something holy; they sensed a connection, even communion, with the Ice Age hunters. Is a sense of the sacred an inherent part of us, something that completes and sustains our humanity, or is it something we have outgrown, like childhood, and replaced with our glittering sciences and the powerful technologies resulting from them? This question has gripped Western culture since the convulsive birth of the modern era five hundred years ago, and it now confronts the world, for technology reaches everywhere and changes everything it touches. At first, new tools simply seem to enhance the existing social order, but we know that is an illusion. Technology transforms in unforeseen ways not only how we live but how we feel and think. It changes how we experience ourselves and relate to others; it changes how society is organized and what it values. The tension between the sacred and the secular fuels contemporary conflicts, from Christian fundamentalists trying to enforce teaching "creation science" in public schools to anti-Western fundamentalists in Islam for whom the idea of a "secular" state proposes a way of life that sets God aside, a form of the sin of idolatry.

John Dewey's *A Common Faith* stands with other twentieth-century classics like William James's *Varieties of Religious Experience*, Paul Tillich's *Dynamics of Faith*, and Martin Buber's *I and Thou*, all of which address this question of spirituality in the modern world. When Dewey gave the 1934 Dwight Huntington Terry Lectures at Yale on the subject of religion, he was in his mid-seventies and known worldwide as the foremost figure in American philosophy, a leader in the movement widely known as pragmatism.[2] Dewey was born in Burlington, Vermont, in 1859, the year Charles Darwin's *Origin of Species* was published. He had a typical boyhood for the time, exploring the Vermont woods and swimming in Lake Champlain. He later remembered that the evangelical Congregationalism of his mother (and New England culture in general) left him with a "sense of divisions and separations," of "isolation of self from the world, of soul from the body, of nature from God," that was "a painful oppression."[3]

Dewey had a quietly questioning mind, not precocious but reflective. Back then it was quite unusual to aspire to be a professional philosopher, but that is where his search led. He attended one of the first graduate programs in philosophy, one newly established at the Johns Hopkins University. There George Sylvester Morris introduced him to absolute idealism, the reigning school of thought in Great Britain and Germany. Absolute idealism holds that all aspects of the world are interwoven parts of a vast, unfolding, all-embracing divine self-consciousness of which we are a part. In contrast to materialism, in which all higher things—consciousness, meaning, value—are regarded as by-products of physical events, idealism argues that ultimate reality grounds our highest values. Physical reality is but part of the picture, and our rational consciousness gives us a better insight into what truly exists. The term for this ultimate reality is "the Absolute." Philosophy's job is to reveal this truth against the limited, partial empirical truths of science that leave our moral values and spiritual aspirations in question. Absolute idealism tries to make sense out of the fragmented world of modernity by finding a unifying, spiritual meaning behind it all. From early on in his career, Dewey was an articulate defender of this view. His innovative thesis was that the emerging science of psychology, as the science of consciousness, could be used to support the central claims of idealism. Psychology would be no new scientific threat to our self-image but, rather, a key to finding transcendent spiritual reality. During this period, however, Darwin's *Origin of Species* was challenging such views, seeing no ultimate purpose or meaning in existence beyond the struggle for survival. Could our spiritual self-image survive the theory of evolution?

Dewey had deftly argued for his "psychological idealism"

in his first book, *Psychology*. But the appearance of William James's *Principles of Psychology* in 1890 shook Dewey to the core. In that massive, brilliant work, James treated the mind from a Darwinian approach; he argued that experience came as a dynamic, flowing process in which the mind was no spectator but a "fighter for ends." Its role was to select certain features, those with most bearing for the organism, and ignore others in order to direct action. Like a heart, hand, or foot, it had a dynamic role in sustaining life. And this concept had philosophical implications. In 1898, James gave a talk, "Philosophical Conceptions and Practical Results," where he argued that our ideas are not "pictures" of the world but plans of action embodied in habits. Inquiry arises when habits are disturbed and seek to regain dynamic equilibrium. So far, James was echoing insights developed by his friend Charles Sanders Peirce.[4] But James went further: philosophical theories are not "world pictures"; they are *world hypotheses* that orient the way we live, and some beliefs, even if unverified, help determine the meaning of the lives we create.[5] The term "pragmatism" summed up this approach. Eventually James's ideas shifted Dewey away from idealism.

In 1894, Dewey moved to the new University of Chicago as the chair and builder of its department of philosophy (which included psychology and pedagogy). He was quickly involved in advancing the new science of psychology on a theoretical and practical level. Practically he became interested in the psychology of education and developmental psychology, setting up his famous Laboratory School that stressed "learning by doing." On a theoretical level, he was solving problems left standing in James's *Principles.* The most notable instance was his substitution of the model of the "circuit of coordination" (known today as a "feedback loop") for James's stimulus-response "reflex-arc." This circuit provides a model of continuous *learning* rather than a simple mechanistic series of causes and effects; it shows how the meaning of experience can change and develop. Dewey began to realize that learning is more important than the traditional philosophical "problem of knowledge," which consists largely of justifying existing beliefs. Other typical problems, such as "How is knowledge possible?" and "How can we know the external world?" are not "problems" at all. Humans are actively involved with the world both biologically and culturally from the moment of birth. We are perpetual learners, and the question should be how we can become *better* learners.

During his appointment at Chicago (1894–1904), Dewey became increasingly reticent about idealism; the subject of religion in his work faded away, to be replaced by an emphasis on education in publications like *School and Society* (1900) and *The Child and the Curriculum* (1902), whose themes eventually culminated in his most influential book, *Democracy and Education* (1916). But a dramatic change can be seen in Dewey's work beginning in 1905, the year he began teaching at Columbia University in New York. He had broken his ties with the University of Chicago in the spring of 1904, when the university administration did not renew the appointment of his wife, Alice, who had been running the Laboratory School. Then, one of his young children had died during a trip to Europe, resulting in enduring inward agony for both parents. During this period of rupture, Dewey had come to question one of the central ideas in Western philosophy held since the days of Parmenides and Plato, that reality was solely revealed by knowledge.[6] In fact, Dewey realized, most experience is not some sort of "experience of knowing." Does experience reveal reality in ways other than knowing? *Being* in pain, for instance, is not the same as *knowing* you are in pain.

This idea becomes clearer if one thinks of "knowledge" as the outcome of an actual process of inquiry. Inquiry arises from *genuine* doubt and seeks to settle that doubt in *actual* conduct or action, as James and Peirce had said. But there are many types of experience that do not call for inquiry at all, experiences that can be taken on their own terms and not reinterpreted as instances of knowledge. While this novel thesis is implicit in some of Dewey's work at Chicago, it fully emerges in 1905 with "The Postulate of Immediate Empiricism." The official break with idealism came the next year in his presidential address to the American Philosophical Association, "Beliefs and Existences," which was followed by "Experience and Objective Idealism," another major critique. There and repeatedly afterward Dewey portrayed idealism as a prime example of "the intellectualist fallacy" of equating the known with reality and of identifying the ideal as reality completely and fully actualized.[7]

Dewey remained at Columbia for the rest of his career. This marks the period during which he emerged as a nationally and internationally known figure, not only as a philosopher but as an advocate of a number of progressive social and political causes (e.g., extending the vote to women and helping to establish such organizations as the American Civil Liberties Union, the American Association of University Professors, and the National Association for the Advancement of Colored People). On the international level, he visited and wrote about the changing political world in the Soviet Union, China, Japan, Turkey, and Mexico. Dewey's major philosophical works begin to appear: *Human Nature and Conduct* (1922), *The Public and Its Problems* (1927), *Art as Experience* (1934), and *Logic: The Theory of Inquiry* (1938). Dewey's masterpiece describing his metaphysics, *Experience and Nature* (1925), also belongs to this period, as do two works concerning religion: *The Quest for Certainty* (1929) and *A Common Faith* (1934).

The Quest for Certainty is a book resulting from Dewey's Gifford Lectures delivered in Edinburgh in 1929. The purpose of this noted lecture series is to address "natural theology," that is, the question of God as approached through science. Dewey's lectures mostly focus on critiquing the traditional philosophical views of knowledge in light of his own instrumentalism, his theory of inquiry. As in *Experience and Nature*, Dewey portrays human life as pervaded by two interweaving themes: chance, transience, loss, defeat, and death, on the one hand, and joy, order, regularity, artful skills, and life, on the other—the "precarious and the stable," as he sums them up. This rhythmic alteration leads to exploring ways to secure transitory goods through developing tools and skills that provide some control over the environment. But there is another story as well: the ardent desire for these goods motivates us to imagine them already "safe and secured," eternally existing in a spiritual realm.

Our human "quest for goods" gets deflected into a "quest for certainty" by thinking that these goods somehow already exist in another, truer world.

For example, Mircea Eliade sees religious rituals as attempts to escape "secular time" for "sacred time." This latter is the time of cosmic origins and beginnings recounted in religious mythology. By connecting with the "time of origins," the "strong time," ritual awakens the powers that can renew the world.[8] This desire to turn precarious goods into assured realities is also reflected in the history of philosophy, from Plato's forms to the Absolute of the idealists to the worship of symbolic logic by analytic philosophers like Bertrand Russell. When this tendency combines with the belief that reality is identical with the known, a bifurcation is made so that two worlds are set up: one the world of change and fallible action, and the other that perfect realm of pure being attained by rational insight. Plato's "divided line" separating Becoming from Being in the *Republic* is a prime example. But the implications of Dewey's argument also clearly apply to most religious theologies that point to an eternal divine realm.

The Quest for Certainty does not explicitly raise the topic of religion until the very last lecture. There Dewey presents a dramatic challenge: What if we realize that ideals belong not to the realm of what is actual, realized, and perfect but instead to the realm of what is possible, so that they have to be realized by action? Though we might lose a false comfort in the security of "eternal values," we would recognize that ideals have to be imagined, struggled for, and constantly reevaluated to become living meanings in human existence.

"The religious attitude," Dewey says, would be "a sense of the possibilities of existence" and "devotion to the cause of these possibilities" (LW 4: 242). What Dewey proposes, in other words, is to replace what might be called a "spirituality of the actual" with a "spirituality of the possible."[9] A Common Faith can be read as a continuation of The Quest for Certainty. Like the Gifford Lectures, the Terry Lectures are devoted to "religion in the light of science and philosophy." Yale's inviting Dewey to deliver the lectures in 1934 was not entirely a surprise. First, there was the tantalizing conclusion of The Quest for Certainty. But there was also a more immediate reason. Dewey had entered into a highly public, controversial debate in The Christian Century, the main magazine for liberal Protestantism in the United States. It began, innocently enough, with Dewey agreeing to write a review of Is There a God? A Conversation. This book sprang from articles by three philosophers who had debated the question in earlier issues of the magazine. But the editors realized they had a hot topic, and Dewey's anticipated review was trumpeted by full-page ads exclaiming "A Journalistic Event of the First Importance."[10] The review, however, was not very positive. In it, Dewey criticizes the debate mainly for its vagueness. Had it been about "The God"—the God of biblical tradition or any one of the recognizable "Gods" of the philosophers (such as Plato's Divine Craftsman, Aristotle's Prime Mover, or Spinoza's infinite rational substance), at least the reader could have fathomed what it was that was supposed to exist or not exist. Debating the existence or non-existence of the "jealous God" of Israel, says Dewey, at least would be "something to get excited about." This is the God of a set of definite theological beliefs, like the seven days of creation, which modern science has challenged and which, as a result, liberal theology has rejected. But what we have is a vague, abstract, open idea of "a" God—one characterized by "the most colorless and indefinite word in the English language." At best this seems to express "a cosmic guarantee for our moral idealism and optimism" or some "objective counterpart to human love and devotion" (LW 9: 215, 217, 219). What is needed, says Dewey, is to cease trying to make God into "a" being, "a single objective existence, a God" *in* the universe beyond the genuine ground of human goods and ideals (LW 9: 220).[11] The controversy did not die down; Max Otto, one of the book's authors, told Dewey, "In the back of my consciousness there has been a smile, most of the time, as I said to myself: I'll bet he didn't know what he was letting himself in for when he agreed to review the debate" (LW 9: 448).

It was this immediate controversy that led the president of Yale, James R. Angell, to invite Dewey to give the Terry Lectures. Then, as now, religion was a topic of intense discussion with numerous points of view. In addition to liberal theologians like those in *Is There a God?* one could find the full spectrum from fundamentalists and conservative theists to liberal theists to militant atheists, like Bertrand Russell and Joseph Wood Krutch. Above all, there was the powerful figure of Reinhold Niebuhr, a Protestant theologian who advocated radical social change, by force if necessary. He aggressively criticized Dewey for a naïve, optimistic view of human nature that did not take sin and evil seriously.[12] Dewey knew that he had to define himself against this background.

Turning directly to *A Common Faith,* we should consider the title first. George Santayana (a philosopher with whom Dewey had crossed swords) judged the book, saying, "'A Common Faith'? A very common faith indeed!"[13] The usual associations of the word "common" are "ordinary, usual, having no special status, unremarkable," as well as "shared." But Dewey has a rather uncommon sense of "common" in mind. In "Creative Democracy—The Task Before Us," a speech given at the celebration of his eightieth birthday, he says, "Democracy as a way of life is controlled by a working faith in the possibilities of human nature. Belief in the Common Man is a familiar article in the democratic creed. That belief is without basis and significance save as it means faith in the potentialities of human nature as that nature is exhibited in every human being regardless of race, color, sex, birth and family, of material or cultural wealth" (LW 14: 226). A "common faith" means a faith in the *potentialities* of human life to become genuinely fulfilled in meaning and value, but only if those potentialities are actualized through action. Dewey is often misread as saying that "ordinary" experience is fine as it is. This misreading is usually followed by a critique of his "optimism." In fact, Dewey did not think things were fine as they were; he saw that the problems of modern society left the best potentialities of most lives unrealized and frustrated. In *Experience and Nature,* commenting on the way we justify some activities as "useful" in the purely utilitarian sense, Dewey agrees that many activities are necessarily like that. But, he adds, we also thoughtlessly call a lot of activities "useful" simply because we do *not* think about their consequences for the quality of human life.

If we were to ask useful for what? we should be obliged to examine their actual consequences, and when we once honestly and fully faced these consequences we should probably find ground for calling such activities detrimental rather than useful. . . . We do not ask for their effect upon the quality of human life and experience. They are useful to make shoes, houses, motor cars, money, and other things which *may* then be put to use; here inquiry and imagination stop. What they also *make* by way of narrowed, embittered and crippled life, of congested, hurried, confused and extravagant life is left in oblivion. But to be useful is to fulfill need. The characteristic human need is for possession and appreciation of the meaning of things, and this need is ignored and unsatisfied in the traditional notion of the useful. (LW 1: 272)

In *Art as Experience,* Dewey points to the arts because they show how the material of ordinary, "common" experience can be cultivated so as to become inherently fulfilling. The materials of existence have the *potentiality* to become enriched with meaning; this does not mean that they *actually* are so. This is what democracy means for Dewey: a way of life that cultivates the possibility for meaningful, value-rich lives. Such a life requires critical intelligence to comprehend the way things are now, imagination to see the way things might be, and a tragic awareness of how fallible our ideals may turn out to be. To see something as "common," for Dewey, is to grasp it *imaginatively* in terms of its *possibilities for growth.* Dewey's use of the word "common" should not be taken to indicate a complacent optimism based on satisfaction with things as they are now. To grasp the possibilities in the present requires creative exploration and struggle.

The three crucial themes Dewey presents in *A Common Faith* are: (1) the distinction between religions and "the religious" as a form of experience, (2) the idea of God as the creative intersection of the ideal or possible and the real or actual, and (3) the infusion of the religious as a pervasive mode of experience into democratic life. Insofar as the "Abrahamic" religions of Judaism, Christianity, and Islam have defined themselves by sets of theological dogmas about the world, they have been challenged by modern science as well as by other religions with dogmas of their own.[14] If by "religions" one means "beliefs," religions conflict not only with science but also with each other. In fact, there is no one thing called "religion," only diverse religions. But what of "the religious" as a quality of experience—as a way in which existence can become fulfilled? (It should be recalled that for Dewey "experience" refers primarily to a way of *living in the world,* not to some "mental" or conscious event.) In fact, states Dewey, established religions often inhibit or prevent people from experiencing "the religious" in their lives. One result is that when people reject the religion in which they were raised, they reject the importance of the religious in living. *It is these people whom Dewey is addressing.*

"The religious" is not a specific type of psychological experience, such as those William James explores in his *Varieties of Religious Experience.* "It denotes attitudes that may be taken toward every object and every proposed end or ideal" (9). The word "attitude" is important. Often people who have mystical experiences think that some truth about reality has been revealed. Dewey urges that we put the question of revealed truth aside and look at the effect such experiences have on the lives of the individuals who undergo them. There is "an adjustment in life, an orientation, that brings with it a sense of security and peace" (12). Dewey is not talking about *particular* forms of adaptation or accommodation to *particular* situations. "Adjustment" is an orientation of "the whole self" to "the world in which we live" or "the Universe." Nature, existence, or "the Universe" is not just what actually is; it includes *all* its possibilities as well. An "adjustment" is "voluntary," but not as a conscious, intended act of volition; it is "a change *of* will conceived as the organic plenitude of our being" (15). So Dewey is talking about a fundamental orientation to existence that arises from the depths of our being, not just the conscious, volitional mind. It engages existence in terms of its possibilities as well as its actualities. It defines an attitude toward life.

Indeed, Dewey himself underwent such a transformative experience as a young high school teacher. His mother had constantly asked him as a child if he was "right with Jesus." Max Eastman reports from an interview with Dewey, "One evening as he sat reading he had what he calls a 'mystic experience.' It was an answer to that question which still worried him: whether he really meant business when he prayed. It was not a very dramatic mystic experience. There was no vision, not even a definable emotion—just a supremely blissful feeling that his worries were over." In Dewey's words, the sense of it was, "What the hell are you worrying about? Everything that's here is here and you can just lie back on it." Dewey added, "I've never had any doubts since then, nor any beliefs. To me faith means not worrying."[15]

Unlike those moments when imagination merely "supervenes" in life, here imagination "intervenes"; it "interpenetrates all the elements of our being" (17). Imagination is necessary because this sort of experience involves "the world" as a totality beyond what we cognitively grasp—it includes both the world and the self in terms of possibilities as well as actualities. Imagination is what engages the possible. "Neither observation, thought, nor practical activity can attain that complete unification of the self which is called a whole" (17). What Dewey is talking about is *not* an object of cognition; it is *not* a result of a conscious act of will; it is *not* a result of "practical activity."[16] It "possesses the will" as an "influx from sources beyond conscious deliberation and purpose" (18–19). What emerges from this is "the authority of an ideal" or "moral faith" (19). It is faith precisely *because* it is not mistaken as an object of cognition, a dogma, or some external ritual practice. It is an *orientation* to an ideal possibility of existence that constitutes who we are and what we value. It can be compared to theologian Paul Tillich's idea of "ultimate concern": "the embracing and centered act of the personality" that integrates the rational and the unconscious, and so is "ecstatic," by standing beyond the narrow ego of the conscious self.[17] This attitude for Dewey is also integrative, so it is not "ecstatic" in the sense of transcending the body or the world or leaving oneself behind. The conscious ego becomes integrated with a larger self-in-the-world. This deep, pervasive sense of connection to nature in its creative depths Dewey calls "natural piety." Natural piety is acknowledgment of the ground of our being-in-nature, the source of all possibilities as well as that in which we live, move, and have our being.[18]

Perhaps this idea can be illustrated with an example taken from the religious life of the Plains tribes of the United States, the ceremony of the calumet, *chanupa,* or "peace pipe." The pipe is one of the most sacred items of Native American culture, for it is what connects a human being to the sacred powers of the world. It is, in the words of Joseph Epes Brown, a "portable altar" that can, upon use, place one at the center of the cosmos. One of its primary uses is to honor the beings of the sky and earth and the four directions of the horizon (usually beginning with the east and moving to the south, west, and north, the "sunwise" motion replicating the journey of the sun). The pipe is smoked, but often after it has been offered first, mouthpiece pointing away, toward the direction or being that one is honoring. The pipe itself when assembled is a living being replicating the human body, with the "heart" of the bowl and "foot" of the stem, and with the burning *kinnikinik*—tobacco and willow bark —representing the living spirit. In the act of smoking, the pipe invites, invokes, and welcomes the living powers of the universe and conveys prayer and respect through the fragrance. *Mitakuye oyasin,* "we are all related," say the Lakota upon completion of the ritual. The ceremony has integrated the individual with the cosmos, with other people, and with other living beings, animal and spiritual. The individual has become both "oriented" and "grounded" in the fullest sense. The "religious" is this *attitude of living.* It is "walking in beauty," as the Diné (Navajo) say.[19]

In the second lecture, "Faith and Its Object," Dewey addresses the conception of God in light of his discussion of "the religious." He asks, "Are the ideals that move us genuinely ideal or are they ideal only in contrast with our present estate? The import of the question extends far. It determines the meaning given to the word 'God'" (39). First of all, what does he mean by "genuinely ideal"? As we have seen, "ideal" means not only "possible" but also "having authority." He takes the question to be: Do we see "God" as "the unity of all ideal ends arousing us to desire and actions," that is, as "having authority" over volition and emotion, to which one is "supremely devoted," or do we think of God as "some kind of Being having prior and therefore non-ideal [that is, actual] existence" (39)? A desired value conceived as a possibility calls one to action, while a value conceived of as an actually realized good—as "non-ideal"—does not. One might think of this ideal as external, but I think Dewey means an ideal that is *enacted as a meaning of our existence,* one that has to be lived and not just externally attained. It is the difference between running for office and living a whole way of life that is expressive of value—one can think of activists like Susan B. Anthony, Jane Addams, and Frederick Douglass, but this way of life can refer to anyone whose life comes to embody an integrative value, such as Ludwig van Beethoven, Albert Einstein, or Pablo Picasso. A dramatic example is that of Morris Dees, founder of the Southern Poverty Law Center, an organization that fights racist and other organized hate groups. Dees was at the beginning of a successful law and publishing career, but a snowstorm in Chicago closed O'Hare Airport, where he was bound, and caused him to spend a night at the airport in Cincinnati. To pass the time, he bought a paperback copy of Clarence Darrow's *The Story of My Life.*

Before daylight I finished Darrow's story of his life. It changed mine forever. I was reading my own thoughts and feelings. Darrow wrote that as a young boy, "not only could I put myself in the other person's place, but I could not avoid doing so. My sympathies always went out to the weak, the suffering, and the poor. Realizing their sorrows, I tried to relieve them in order that I might be relieved . . ." . . . Once freed from the restraints of the corporate world and able to follow his conscience, Darrow undertook cases that made legal history in the fight for human dignity and justice for the powerless. I read about those cases all night. . . . On the flight to Chicago the next morning I thought a lot about Clarence Darrow. . . . When my plane landed in Chicago, I was ready to take that step and to speak out for my black friends who were still "disenfranchised." . . . I had made up my mind. I would sell the company as soon as possible and specialize in civil rights law. All the things in my life that had brought me to this point, all the pulls and tugs of my conscience, found a singular peace.[20]

Dees sold his publishing business and founded the SPLC, fully aware that he would become a target for the rest of his life. In all these instances, the individuals did not so much "make" a choice to be who they are as they *realized* who they are. The choice made them.

In this sense, God is a "unification of ideal values that is essentially imaginative in origin" (40). For Dewey, imagination is the ability to grasp possibilities—it is seeing the actual in the light of the possible. It should not be thought of as something "imaginary" or "illusory" or even as a "faculty of the mind." When humans grasped how to make fire, an existential possibility *in the world* was actualized that changed the basic relation of our species to the environment. For Dewey, possibilities are as much part of nature as we are. To conceive of them as "mental" replicates a dualistic way of thinking that Dewey regards as part of the problem we have inherited from the birth of modernity. Dewey's view of imagination, then, is "ecological," not "mental." When imagination achieves an integrated unification of our ideals, our *lives*—not our "minds"—become enactments *in the world* of an integrated self; we are living the life of someone we want to be, and who we want to be is someone whose life is pervaded by these ideals. They genuinely *guide* us from within.

God, then, for Dewey is an immanent creative possibility in existence, not "a" being that transcends nature—for nature's possibilities are as natural as its actualities. Dewey says, "The ideal itself has its roots in natural conditions; it emerges when the imagination idealizes existence by laying hold of the possibilities offered to thought and action" (44). These possibilities are not just the "stuff of dreams," either. They "are made out of the hard stuff of the world of physical and social experience" (45). Dewey then proceeds to make one of his most controversial pronouncements in the entire book: "It is this *active* relation between ideal and actual to which I would give the name 'God,'" though he adds, "I would not insist that the name *must* be given" (47).

This statement startled both Dewey's followers and his critics, and the vortex of criticism that surrounded Dewey upon publication of *A Common Faith* centered on this claim. Dewey's allies, who identified naturalism with atheism, felt betrayed. Corliss Lamont, reviewing the book for the Marxist periodical *New Masses,* titled his essay "John Dewey Capitulates to 'God.'"[21] Liberal theists, like Henry Nelson Wieman (one of the authors of *Is There a God?*), thought that they had triumphed: Dewey *was* a theist all along! But Dewey himself had clearly stated why he thought the term "God" should be used: it was to challenge "aggressive" or "militant atheism." This sort of atheism, he observes, shares something with the theistic positions it rejects: "the exclusive preoccupation . . . with man in isolation" (49). Both positions see human beings as separate from nature, atheism giving us a supernatural status *above* nature and theism pitting us *against* nature. "Militant atheism is also affected by lack of natural piety. The ties binding man to nature that poets have always celebrated are passed over lightly. The attitude taken is often that of man living in an indifferent and hostile world and issuing blasts of defiance. A religious attitude, however, needs the sense of a connection of man, in the way of both dependence and support, with the enveloping world that the imagination feels is a universe" (49).[22] In contemporary language, Dewey could be said to advocate an "ecological spirituality." Traditional Christianity and Cartesian dualism see the human soul or mind as something apart from nature, either transcending it or mastering it through science. This alienation has not been helpful in the past and is positively dangerous now as we face the consequences of our ecological negligence and greed. Dewey's "militant atheists" are still present in figures like Richard Dawkins or the late Christopher Hitchens.

The third main idea Dewey discusses is the social dimension of religions and the religious. Most societies have been pervaded by religion as a whole way of life. One thinks of tribal societies, for whom the whole way of life *is* "religion," or of communities defined by one religion, such as Medieval Christendom or the life of the Jewish villages or *shtetels* of eastern Europe. In these instances one is raised in a religion; there is no question of "choosing" it. Today, however, modern societies tend to be secular, offering a variety of religions from which to choose or not to choose. Religions are aspects of society, not a pervasive, defining collective way of life. Dewey sees this shift as more significant than the intellectual challenge modern science brings to old theological beliefs. A whole way of existence, not just a set of beliefs, has been altered. As noted, the very idea of a "secular civilization" threatens Islamic as well as Jewish and Christian fundamentalists. This is where Dewey's distinction between "religions" and "the religious" hits home. The religious *way of life* is felt to be challenged because it is bound up with some "religion" as a *set of beliefs* that is questioned. Dewey asks: "What would be the consequences upon the values of human association if intrinsic and immanent satisfactions and opportunities were clearly held to and cultivated with the ardor and the devotion that have at times marked historic religions?" (66). He points to the possibilities of social transformation so that the basic conditions for shared lives of meaningful growth are increasingly available, even though "vested interests, interests vested with power, are powerfully on the side of the *status quo*" (71). What was true in 1934 is truer today, as multinational corporations protect vast wealth for a few and acquire political influence by pouring huge sums into elections. Dewey's point is that this is not the way it has to be—any more than slavery or the subjection of women had to be. When those conditions changed, new possibilities began to open up, albeit slowly and with continued struggle. One way of defining democracy could be that it seeks to provide every person with the most meaningful choices possible, which means imagining what those possibilities might be.

The most important implication of the idea of the religious in social existence lies in education. Dewey remarks at the beginning of *Democracy and Education* that everyone dies—but not everyone all at once. Thus, culture can be passed on from generation to generation. There can be transmission and cumulative learning. Moreover, what we inherit from the past can develop and change. We may like to think we are isolated individuals; in fact, we are the inheritors of the whole range of human experience as embodied and passed on in culture. The three French cave explorers who discovered Chauvet Cave were not physically different from the humans who painted the images of the animals on its walls thirty thousand years ago. What separates them from, as well as connects them to, those archaic people is the transmission of culture. In teaching, we are giving others a *world* to inhabit, explore, and develop. This must not be done uncritically; much of the past is a dubious burden. But knowing that we have been blind in the past is one of the most important lessons to pass on, for it makes us aware of our inherent finitude—the "tragic wisdom" embodied in the Greek saying *gnōthi seauton*, "Know thyself."

Finally, we can raise some questions concerning *A Common Faith*. Though Dewey's natural piety stresses acknowledging nature, and not human nature alone, as the source of value, does he adequately appreciate how awe arises from what indeed does "transcend" or go beyond us? The capacity for reverence is part of what makes us human. The painters who left the stunning images of mammoths and bison in the caves were not just expressing their physical connection to the game animals or trying to overpower them by magic. The images express a sense of awe, holiness, and gratitude. Are we losing even the *ability* to experience reverence, aside from whether we live with it as a pervasive sense of existence? In *Reverence: Renewing a Forgotten Virtue*, Robert Paul Woodruff worries that he is describing a dying but crucial virtue.[23] A culture devoted to egoistic materialism cannot meet our deepest needs. So how might a way of democratic life pervaded by a sense of the religious be achieved? How can we cultivate awe, gratitude, and a sense of the holy democratically?

Does Dewey, though no naïve optimist, place too much confidence in science and technology even if they are used to enrich human existence? He acknowledges that the main problem of modernity is that the power science has given us has not been matched by the wisdom to use it. Dewey placed his hope in the power of education. Is this enough? Before we dismiss the idea, we should remember what minimal resources we allocate to education. What if even half as much as we spend on the military were spent on education? But would even that be enough to counteract the influences bombarding young and old from all sides? Intelligence may be passed on, but so can lies, stupidity, greed, and hate. And what of the personal needs of individuals to meet the crises and tragedies of life? Is a "God of possibility" enough? Nor does Dewey have much to say about inwardness and the individual cultivation of spirituality.

Dewey's *A Common Faith* is a rich and provocative text that provides an original response to the question of the role of the religious dimension of human experience in a world that has been transformed by science. While it may call forth some of the questions listed above, it may also indicate one way to explore an "ecological spirituality" that does not succumb to the dualistic and supernatural dogmas that have defined Western religion in the past.[24] It is still a vital text that speaks to us.

Notes

1. See David Lewis-Williams, *The Mind in the Cave* (London: Thames & Hudson, 2002), p. 17.

2. Dewey called his philosophy "cultural naturalism." Pragmatism—or "instrumentalism," as he preferred to call it—refers to only part of that philosophy, the theory of inquiry. In a letter to Corliss Lamont, Dewey wrote: "I have come to think of my own position as cultural or humanistic Naturalism. Naturalism, properly interpreted, seems to me a more adequate term than Humanism. Of course I have always limited my use of 'instrumentalism' to my theory of thinking and knowledge; the word 'pragmatism' I have used very little, and then with reserves" (Dewey to Corliss Lamont, Sept. 6, 1940, cited in Corliss Lamont, "New Light on Dewey's *Common Faith*," *The Journal of Philosophy* 58, no. 1 [1961], p. 26).

3. John Dewey, "From Absolutism to Experimentalism," in *The Later Works*, vol. 5, ed. Jo Ann Boydston (Carbondale: Southern Illinois University Press, 1984), p. 153. This series, including *The Early Works* and *The Middle Works*, is the standard edition of Dewey's writings and henceforth will be cited in text and notes with the customary abbreviation (EW, MW, LW) followed by volume and page number, e.g., LW 5: 153.

4. See Peirce's famous essays "The Fixation of Belief" and "How to Make Our Ideas Clear," both of which may be found in *The Essential Peirce*, 2 vols. (Indianapolis: University of Indiana Press, 1992, 1998).

5. These ideas are developed by James in *The Will to Believe* (1897), *Pragmatism* (1908), and *The Varieties of Religious Experience* (1903). Peirce's own application of pragmatism to the question of religion can be found in his essays "Evolutionary Love" (1893) and "The Neglected Argument for the Reality of God" (1903). These also may be found in *The Essential Peirce*.

6. Dewey's questioning of this assumption may be compared to alternatives explored by Friedrich Nietzsche, Henri Bergson, and Martin Heidegger.

7. See, for example, *The Quest for Certainty*, LW 4: 234–35. See MW 3 for Dewey's article and critical responses. "The Intellectualist Criterion of Truth" develops the criticism of the "Intellectualist Fallacy," and "What Pragmatism Means by Practical" (both in MW 4) develops the positive alternative, that action engages reality as possibility.

8. See studies by Mircea Eliade: *Myth and Reality* (Prospect Heights, Ill.: Waveland Press, 1998), *The Myth of the Eternal Return: Cosmos and History* (Princeton: Princeton University Press, 2005), and *The Sacred and Profane: The Nature of Religion* (New York: Harcourt Brace Jovanovich, 1987).

9. See my essay "The Spirituality of the Possible in John Dewey's *A Common Faith*," in Thomas M. Alexander, *The Human Eros: Eco-Ontology and the Aesthetics of Existence* (New York: Fordham University Press, 2013).

10. See Dewey's review and supporting textual material and discussion in LW 9: 213–22 and 445–56. (LW 9 also contains the critical edition of *A Common Faith*.) For discussion see Steven C. Rockefeller, *John Dewey: Religious Faith and Democratic Humanism* (New York: Columbia University Press, 1991), p. 512 ff., and William Shea, *The Naturalists and the Supernatural* (Macon, Ga.: Mercer University Press, 1984). A synopsis of Rockefeller's views can be found in his essay "Dewey's Philosophy of Religious Experi-

ence," in *Reading Dewey: Interpretations for a Postmodern Generation,* ed. Larry A. Hickman (Indianapolis: Indiana University Press, 1998), pp. 124–25.

11. Theologian Paul Tillich also rejects the idea of God as "a being" among the collection of beings *in* the universe; God is, for him, the "ground of Being" and is symbolized for each of us as our "object of ultimate concern." See his *The Dynamics of Faith* (New York: Harper & Row, 1957), especially chaps. 1 and 6.

12. See Rockefeller, *John Dewey,* pp. 461–62, 484–85, and 523–24.

13. John Herman Randall, Jr., "The Religion of Shared Experience," in *Philosophy after Darwin,* ed. Beth J. Singer (New York: Columbia University Press, 1977), p. 241.

14. Many religions, however, are not defined by beliefs or dogmas. Joseph Campbell, a scholar of world religions, told the story of a Westerner asking a Japanese Shinto priest what his "theology" was. The priest looked puzzled and replied, "We don't have a theology. We dance." See Stephen and Robin Larsen, *A Fire in the Mind: A Life of Joseph Campbell* (New York: Anchor Books, 1991), p. 438.

15. Max Eastman, "John Dewey," *Atlantic* 168, no. 6 (December 1941), p. 673. See discussion in Rockefeller, *John Dewey,* pp. 67–68. A very similar experience happened to the Transcendentalist Margaret Fuller. See Robert Richardson, *Emerson: The Mind on Fire* (Berkeley: University of California Press, 1995), pp. 237–38. Victor Kestenbaum provides a sensitive, probing analysis of this rather neglected side of Dewey in "Faith and the Unseen," in his *The Grace and Severity of the Ideal* (Chicago: University of Chicago Press, 202), pp. 175–99.

16. This is why Dewey's theory of the pervasive, qualitative dimension of all experience, including practical and cognitive experience, is crucial for grasping his thought. See Douglas Anderson's "John Dewey's Sensible Mysticism," in his *Philosophy Americana* (New York: Fordham University Press, 2006), pp. 129–41.

17. Tillich, *Dynamics of Faith,* p. 6.

18. The phrase "natural piety" comes from Wordsworth's "My Heart Leaps Up" (also known as "The Rainbow"; it is quoted in part at the beginning of "Ode: Intimations of Immortality"). The idea is developed at length in George Santayana's *The Life of Reason: Reason in Religion* (New York:

Scribner's, 1905), chap. 10. See discussion in Rockefeller, *John Dewey,* pp. 495–96.

19. See Joseph Epes Brown (with Black Elk), *The Sacred Pipe,* 3rd ed. (Norman: University of Oklahoma Press, 1989), and his essay "The Spiritual Legacy," in *The Spiritual Legacy of the American Indian* (New York: Crossroad, 1991), as well as Hartley Burr Alexander, *The World's Rim* (Lincoln: University of Nebraska Press, 1953), chap. 1. For a sensitive, fascinating discussion of the Navajo concept of "walking in beauty" (*sa'a naghai bik'e hozho*), see John R. Farella, *The Main Stalk: A Synthesis of Navajo Philosophy* (Tuscon: University of Arizona Press, 1984), chap. 5.

20. Morris Dees with Steve Fiffer, *A Lawyer's Journey: The Morris Dees Story* (Chicago: American Bar Association, 2001), pp. 95–97.

21. The critical approach that seeks to reject or marginalize Dewey's philosophy of religious experience is best represented by Michael Eldridge's *Transforming Experience: John Dewey's Cultural Instrumentalism* (Nashville: Vanderbilt University Press, 1998), chap. 5. Eldridge says, "I think Dewey's willingness to use the language of faith and even the word 'God' is counterproductive" (p. 168).

22. Compare: "*A Common Faith* was not addressed to those who are content with traditions in which 'metaphysical' is substantially identical with 'supernatural.' It was addressed to those who have abandoned supernaturalism, and who on that account are reproached by traditionalists for having turned their backs on everything religious. The book was an attempt to show such persons that they still have within their experience all the elements which give the religious attitude its value." *The Philosophy of John Dewey,* ed. Paul Schilpp (Tudor Publishing: New York, 1939), p. 597.

23. New York: Oxford University Press, 2002.

24. See Steven Rockefeller's exploration of this issue, *John Dewey,* pp. 532–33.

I

RELIGION VERSUS THE RELIGIOUS

Never before in history has mankind been so much of two minds, so divided into two camps, as it is today. Religions have traditionally been allied with ideas of the supernatural, and often have been based upon explicit beliefs about it. Today there are many who hold that nothing worthy of being called religious is possible apart from the supernatural. Those who hold this belief differ in many respects. They range from those who accept the dogmas and sacraments of the Greek and Roman Catholic church as the only sure means of access to the supernatural to the theist or mild deist. Between them are the many Protestant denominations who think the Scriptures, aided by a pure conscience, are adequate avenues to supernatural truth and power. But they agree in one point: the necessity for a Supernatural Being and for an immortality that is beyond the power of nature.

The opposed group consists of those who think the advance of culture and science has completely discredited the supernatural and with it all religions that were allied with belief in it. But they go beyond this point. The extremists in this group believe that with elimination of the supernatural not only must historic religions be dismissed but with them everything of a religious nature. When historical knowledge has discredited the claims made for the supernatural character of the persons said to have founded historic religions; when the supernatural inspiration attributed to literatures held sacred has been riddled, and when anthropological and psychological knowledge has disclosed the all-too-human source from which religious beliefs and practices have sprung, everything religious must, they say, also go.

There is one idea held in common by these two opposite groups: identification of the religious with the supernatural. The question I shall raise in these chapters concerns the ground for and the consequences of this identification: its reasons and its value. In the discussion I shall develop another conception of the nature of the religious phase of experience, one that separates it from the supernatural and the things that have grown up about it. I shall try to show that these derivations are encumbrances and that what is genuinely religious will undergo an emancipation when it is relieved from them; that then, for the first time, the religious aspect of experience will be free to develop freely on its own account.

This view is exposed to attack from both the other camps. It goes contrary to traditional religions, including those that have the greatest hold upon the religiously minded today. The view announced will seem to them to cut the vital nerve of the religious element itself in taking away the basis upon which traditional religions and institutions have been founded. From the other side, the position I am taking seems like a timid halfway position, a concession and compromise unworthy of thought that is thoroughgoing. It is regarded as a view entertained from mere tendermindedness, as an emotional hangover from childhood indoctrination, or even as a manifestation of a desire to avoid disapproval and curry favor.

The heart of my point, as far as I shall develop it in this first section, is that there is a difference between religion, *a* religion, and the religious; between anything that may be denoted by a noun substantive and the quality of experience that is designated by an adjective. It is not easy to find a definition of religion in the substantive sense that wins general acceptance. However, in the *Oxford Dictionary* I find the following: "Recognition on the part of man of some unseen higher power as having control of his destiny and as being entitled to obedience, reverence and worship."

This particular definition is less explicit in assertion of the supernatural character of the higher unseen power than are others that might be cited. It is, however, surcharged with implications having their source in ideas connected with the belief in the supernatural, characteristic of historic religions. Let us suppose that one familiar with the history of religions, including those called primitive, compares the definition with the variety of known facts and by means of the comparison sets out to determine just what the definition means. I think he will be struck by three facts that reduce the terms of the definition to such a low common denominator that little meaning is left. He will note that the "unseen powers" referred to have been conceived in a multitude of incompatible ways. Eliminating the differences, nothing is left beyond the bare reference to something unseen and powerful. This has been conceived as the vague and undefined Mana of the Melanesians; the Kami of primitive Shintoism; the fetish of the Africans; spirits, having some human properties, that pervade natural places and animate natural forces; the ultimate and impersonal principle of Buddhism; the unmoved mover of Greek thought; the gods and semi-divine heroes of the Greek and Roman Pantheons; the personal and loving Providence of Christianity, omnipotent, and limited by a corresponding evil power; the arbitrary Will of Moslemism; the supreme legislator and judge of deism. And these are but a few of the outstanding varieties of ways in which the invisible power has been conceived.

There is no greater similarity in the ways in which obedience and reverence have been expressed. There has been worship of animals, of ghosts, of ancestors, phallic worship, as well as of a Being of dread power and of love and wisdom. Reverence has been expressed in the human sacrifices of the Peruvians and Aztecs; the sexual orgies of some Oriental religions; exorcisms and ablutions; the offering of the humble and contrite mind of the Hebrew prophet, the elaborate rituals of the Greek and Roman Churches. Not even sacrifice has been uniform; it is highly sublimated in Protestant denominations and in Moslemism. Where it has existed it has taken all kinds of forms and been directed to a great variety of powers and spirits. It has been used for expiation, for propitiation and for buying special favors. There is no conceivable purpose for which rites have not been employed. Finally, there is no discernible unity in the moral motivations appealed to and utilized. They have been as far apart as fear of lasting torture, hope of enduring bliss in which sexual enjoyment has sometimes been a conspicuous element; mortification of the flesh and extreme asceticism; prostitution and chastity; wars to extirpate the unbeliever; persecution to convert or punish the unbeliever, and philanthropic zeal; servile acceptance of imposed dogma, along with brotherly love and aspiration for a reign of justice among men.

I have, of course, mentioned only a sparse number of the facts which fill volumes in any well-stocked library. It may be asked by those who do not like to look upon the darker side of the history of religions why the darker facts should be brought up. We all know that civilized man has a background of bestiality and superstition and that these elements are still with us. Indeed, have not some religions, including the most influential forms of Christianity, taught that the heart of man is totally corrupt? How could the course of religion in its entire sweep not be marked by practices that are shameful in their cruelty and lustfulness, and by beliefs that are degraded and intellectually incredible? What else than what we find could be expected, in the case of people having little knowledge and no secure method of knowing; with primitive institutions, and with so little control of natural forces that they lived in a constant state of fear? I gladly admit that historic religions have been relative to the conditions of social culture in which peoples lived. Indeed, what I am concerned with is to press home the logic of this method of disposal of outgrown traits of past religions. Beliefs and practices in a religion that now prevails are by this logic relative to the present state of culture. If so much flexibility has obtained in the past regarding an unseen power, the way it affects human destiny, and the attitudes we are to take toward it, why should it be assumed that change in conception and action has now come to an end? The logic involved in getting rid of inconvenient aspects of past religions compels us to inquire how much in religions now accepted are survivals from outgrown cultures. It compels us to ask what conception of unseen powers and our relations to them would be consonant with the best achievements and aspirations of the present. It demands that in imagination we wipe the slate clean and start afresh by asking what would be the idea of the unseen, of the manner of its control over us and the ways in which reverence and obedience would be manifested, if whatever is basically religious in experience had the opportunity to express itself free from all historic encumbrances.

So we return to the elements of the definition that has been given. What boots it to accept, in defense of the universality of religion, a definition that applies equally to the most savage and degraded beliefs and practices that have related to unseen powers and to noble ideals of a religion having the greatest share of moral content? There are two points involved. One of them is that there is nothing left worth preserving in the notions of unseen powers, controlling human destiny to which obedience, reverence and worship are due, if we glide silently over the nature that has been attributed to the powers, the radically diverse ways in which they have been supposed to control human destiny, and in which submission and awe have been manifested. The other point is that when we begin to select, to choose, and say that some present ways of thinking about the unseen powers are better than others; that the reverence shown by a free and self-respecting human being is better than the servile obedience rendered to an arbitrary power by frightened men; that we should believe that control of human destiny is exercised by a wise and loving spirit rather than by madcap ghosts or sheer force—when I say, we begin to choose, we have entered upon a road that has not yet come to an end. We have reached a point that invites us to proceed farther.

For we are forced to acknowledge that concretely there is no such thing as religion in the singular. There is only a multitude of religions. "Religion" is a strictly collective term and the collection it stands for is not even of the kind illustrated in textbooks of logic. It has not the unity of a regiment or assembly but that of any miscellaneous aggregate. Attempts to prove the universality prove too much or too little. It is probable that religions have been universal in the sense that all the peoples we know anything about have had *a* religion. But the differences among them are so great and so shocking that any common element that can be extracted is meaningless. The idea that religion is universal proves too little in that the older apologists for Christianity seem to have been better advised than some modern ones in condemning every religion but one as an impostor, as at bottom some kind of demon worship or at any rate a superstitious figment. Choice among religions is imperative, and the necessity for choice leaves nothing of any force in the argument from universality. Moreover, when once we enter upon the road of choice, there is at once presented a possibility not yet generally realized.

For the historic increase of the ethical and ideal content of religions suggests that the process of purification may be carried further. It indicates that further choice is imminent in which certain values and functions in experience may be selected. This possibility is what I had in mind in speaking of the difference between the religious and a religion. I am not proposing a religion, but rather the emancipation of elements and outlooks that may be called religious. For the moment we have a religion, whether that of the Sioux Indian or of Judaism or of Christianity, that moment the ideal factors in experience that may be called religious take on a load that is not inherent in them, a load of current beliefs and of institutional practices that are irrelevant to them.

I can illustrate what I mean by a common phenomenon in contemporary life. It is widely supposed that a person who does not accept any religion is thereby shown to be a non-religious person. Yet it is conceivable that the present depression in religion is closely connected with the fact that religions now prevent, because of their weight of historic encumbrances, the religious quality of experience from coming to consciousness and finding the expression that is appropriate to present conditions, intellectual and moral. I believe that such is the case. I believe that many persons are so repelled from what exists as a religion by its intellectual and moral implications, that they are not even aware of attitudes in themselves that if they came to fruition would be genuinely religious. I hope that this remark may help make clear what I mean by the distinction between "religion" as a noun substantive and "religious" as adjectival.

To be somewhat more explicit, a religion (and as I have just said there is no such thing as religion in general) always signifies a special body of beliefs and practices having some kind of institutional organization, loose or tight. In contrast, the adjective "religious" denotes nothing in the way of a specifiable entity, either institutional or as a system of beliefs. It does not denote anything to which one can specifically point as one can point to this and that historic religion or existing church. For it does not denote anything that can exist by itself or that can be organized into a particular and distinctive form of existence. It denotes attitudes that may be taken toward every object and every proposed end or ideal.

Before, however, I develop my suggestion that realization of the distinction just made would operate to emancipate the religious quality from encumbrances that now smother or limit it, I must refer to a position that in some respects is similar in words to the position I have taken, but that in fact is a whole world removed from it. I have several times used the phrase "religious elements of experience." Now at present there is much talk, especially in liberal circles, of religious experience as vouching for the authenticity of certain beliefs and the desirability of certain practices, such as particular forms of prayer and worship. It is even asserted that religious experience is the ultimate basis of religion itself. The gulf between this position and that which I have taken is what I am now concerned to point out.

Those who hold to the notion that there is a definite kind of experience which is itself religious, by that very fact make out of it something specific, as a kind of experience that is marked off from experience as æsthetic, scientific, moral, political; from experience as companionship and friendship. But "religious" as a quality of experience signifies something that may belong to all these experiences. It is the polar opposite of some type of experience that can exist by itself. The distinction comes out clearly when it is noted that the concept of this distinct kind of experience is used to validate a belief in some special kind of object and also to justify some special kind of practice.

For there are many religionists who are now dissatisfied with the older "proofs" of the existence of God, those that go by the name of ontological, cosmological and teleological. The cause of the dissatisfaction is perhaps not so much the arguments that Kant used to show the insufficiency of these alleged proofs, as it is the growing feeling that they are too formal to offer any support to religion in action. Anyway, the dissatisfaction exists. Moreover, these religionists are moved by the rise of the experimental method in other fields. What is more natural and proper, accordingly, than that they should affirm they are just as good empiricists as anybody else—indeed, as good as the scientists themselves? As the latter rely upon certain kinds of experience to prove the existence of certain kinds of objects, so the religionists rely upon a certain kind of experience to prove the existence of the object of religion, especially the supreme object, God. The discussion may be made more definite by introducing, at this point, a particular illustration of this type of reasoning. A writer says: "I broke down from overwork and soon came to the verge of nervous prostration. One morning after a long and sleepless night . . . I resolved to stop drawing upon myself so continuously and begin drawing upon God. I determined to set apart a quiet time every day in which I could relate my life to its ultimate source, regain the consciousness that in God I live, move and have my being. That was thirty years ago. Since then I have had literally not one hour of darkness or despair."

This is an impressive record. I do not doubt its authenticity nor that of the experience related. It illustrates a religious aspect of experience. But it illustrates also the use of that quality to carry a superimposed load of a particular religion. For having been brought up in the Christian religion, its subject interprets it in the terms of the personal God characteristic of that religion. Taoists, Buddhists, Moslems, persons of no religion including those who reject all supernatural influence and power, have had experiences similar in their effect. Yet another author commenting upon the passage says: "The religious expert can be more sure that this God exists than he can of either the cosmological God of speculative surmise or the Christlike God involved in the validity of moral optimism," and goes on to add that such experiences "mean that God the savior, the power that gives victory over sin on certain conditions that man can fulfill, is an existent, accessible and scientifically knowable reality." It should be clear that this inference is sound only if the conditions, of whatever sort, that produce the effect are called "God." But most readers will take the inference to mean that the existence of a particular Being, of the type called "God" in the Christian religion, is proved by a method akin to that of experimental science.

In reality, the only thing that can be said to be "proved" is the existence of some complex of conditions that have operated to effect an adjustment in life, an orientation, that brings with it a sense of security and peace. The particular interpretation given to this complex of conditions is not inherent in the experience itself. It is derived from the culture with which a particular person has been imbued. A fatalist will give one name to it; a Christian Scientist another, and the one who rejects all supernatural being still another. The determining factor in the interpretation of the experience is the particular doctrinal apparatus into which a person has been inducted. The emotional deposit connected with prior teaching floods the whole situation. It may readily confer upon the experience such a peculiarly sacred preciousness that all inquiry into its causation is barred. The stable outcome is so invaluable that the cause to which it is referred is usually nothing but a reduplication of the thing that has occurred, plus some name that has acquired a deeply emotional quality.

The intent of this discussion is not to deny the genuineness of the result nor its importance in life. It is not, save incidentally, to point out the possibility of a purely naturalistic explanation of the event. My purpose is to indicate what happens when religious experience is already set aside as something *sui generis*. The actual religious quality in the experience described is the *effect* produced, the better adjustment in life and its conditions, not the manner and cause of its production. The way in which the experience operated, its function, determines its religious value. If the reorientation actually occurs, it, and the sense of security and stability accompanying it, are forces on their own account. It takes place in different persons in a multitude of ways. It is sometimes brought about by devotion to a cause; sometimes by a passage of poetry that opens a new perspective; sometimes as was the case with Spinoza—deemed an atheist in his day—through philosophical reflection.

The difference between an experience having a religious force because of what it does in and to the processes of living and religious experience as a separate kind of thing gives me occasion to refer to a previous remark. If this function were rescued through emancipation from dependence upon specific types of beliefs and practices, from those elements that constitute a religion, many individuals would find that experiences having the force of bringing about a better, deeper and enduring adjustment in life are not so rare and infrequent as they are commonly supposed to be. They occur frequently in connection with many significant moments of living. The idea of invisible powers would take on the meaning of all the conditions of nature and human association that support and deepen the sense of values which carry one through periods of darkness and despair to such an extent that they lose their usual depressive character.

I do not suppose for many minds the dislocation of the religious from a religion is easy to effect. Tradition and custom, especially when emotionally charged, are a part of the habits that have become one with our very being. But the possibility of the transfer is demonstrated by its actuality. Let us then for the moment drop the term "religious," and ask what are the attitudes that lend deep and enduring support to the processes of living. I have, for example, used the words "adjustment" and "orientation." What do they signify?

While the words "accommodation," "adaptation," and "adjustment" are frequently employed as synonyms, attitudes exist that are so different that for the sake of clear thought they should be discriminated. There are conditions we meet that cannot be changed. If they are particular and limited, we modify our own particular attitudes in accordance with them. Thus we accommodate ourselves to changes in weather, to alterations in income when we have no other recourse. When the external conditions are lasting we become inured, habituated, or, as the process is now often called, conditioned. The two main traits of this attitude, which I should like to call accommodation, are that it affects *particular* modes of conduct, not the entire self, and that the process is mainly *passive*. It may, however, become general and then it becomes fatalistic resignation or submission. There are other attitudes toward the environment that are also particular but that are more active. We re-act against conditions and endeavor to change them to meet our wants and demands. Plays in a foreign language are "adapted" to meet the needs of an American audience. A house is rebuilt to suit changed conditions of the household; the telephone is invented to serve the demand for speedy communication at a distance; dry soils are irrigated so that they may bear abundant crops. Instead of accommodating ourselves to conditions, we modify conditions so that they will be accommodated to our wants and purposes. This process may be called adaptation.

Now both of these processes are often called by the more general name of adjustment. But there are also changes in ourselves in relation to the world in which we live that are much more inclusive and deep seated. They relate not to this and that want in relation to this and that condition of our surroundings, but pertain to our being in its entirety. Because of their scope, this modification of ourselves is enduring. It lasts through any amount of vicissitude of circumstances, internal and external. There is a composing and harmonizing of the various elements of our being such that, in spite of changes in the special conditions that surround us, these conditions are also arranged, settled, in relation to us. This attitude includes a note of submission. But it is voluntary, not externally imposed; and as voluntary it is something more than a mere Stoical resolution to endure unperturbed throughout the buffetings of fortune. It is more outgoing, more ready and glad, than the latter attitude, and it is more active than the former. And in calling it voluntary, it is not meant that it depends upon a particular resolve or volition. It is a change *of* will conceived as the organic plenitude of our being, rather than any special change *in* will.

It is the claim of religions that they effect this generic and enduring change in attitude. I should like to turn the statement around and say that whenever this change takes place there is a definitely religious attitude. It is not *a* religion that brings it about, but when it occurs, from whatever cause and by whatever means, there is a religious outlook and function. As I have said before, the doctrinal or intellectual apparatus and the institutional accretions that grow up are, in a strict sense, adventitious to the intrinsic quality of such experiences. For they are affairs of the traditions of the culture with which individuals are inoculated. Mr. Santayana has connected the religious quality of experience with the imaginative, as that is expressed in poetry. "Religion and poetry," he says, "are identical in essence, and differ merely in the way in which they are attached to practical affairs. Poetry is called religion when it intervenes in life, and religion, when it merely supervenes upon life, is seen to be nothing but poetry." The difference between intervening *in* and supervening *upon* is as important as is the identity set forth. Imagination may play upon life or it may enter profoundly into it. As Mr. Santayana puts it, "poetry has a universal and a moral function," for "its highest power lies in its relevance to the ideals and purposes of life." Except as it intervenes, "all observation is observation of brute fact, all discipline is mere repression, until these facts digested and this discipline embodied in humane impulses become the starting point for a creative movement of the imagination, the firm basis for ideal constructions in society, religion, and art."

If I may make a comment upon this penetrating insight of Mr. Santayana, I would say that the difference between imagination that only supervenes and imagination that intervenes is the difference between one that completely interpenetrates all the elements of our being and one that is interwoven with only special and partial factors. There actually occurs extremely little observation of brute facts merely for the sake of the facts, just as there is little discipline that is repression and nothing but repression. Facts are usually observed with reference to some practical end and purpose, and that end is presented only imaginatively. The most repressive discipline has some end in view to which there is at least imputed an ideal quality; otherwise it is purely sadistic. But in such cases of observation and discipline imagination is limited and partial. It does not extend far; it does not permeate deeply and widely.

The connection between imagination and the harmonizing of the self is closer than is usually thought. The idea of a whole, whether of the whole personal being or of the world, is an imaginative, not a literal, idea. The limited world of our observation and reflection becomes the Universe only through imaginative extension. It cannot be apprehended in knowledge nor realized in reflection. Neither observation, thought, nor practical activity can attain that complete unification of the self which is called a whole. The *whole* self is an ideal, an imaginative projection. Hence the idea of a thoroughgoing and deep-seated harmonizing of the self with the Universe (as a name for the totality of conditions with which the self is connected) operates only through imagination—which is one reason why this composing of the self is not voluntary in the sense of an act of special volition or resolution. An "adjustment" possesses the will rather than is its express product. Religionists have been right in thinking of it as an influx from sources beyond conscious deliberation and purpose—a fact that helps explain, psychologically, why it has so generally been attributed to a supernatural source and that, perhaps, throws some light upon the reference of it by William James to unconscious factors. And it is pertinent to note that the unification of the self throughout the ceaseless flux of what it does, suffers, and achieves, cannot be attained in terms of itself. The self is always directed toward something beyond itself and so its own unification depends upon the idea of the integration of the shifting scenes of the world into that imaginative totality we call the Universe.

The intimate connection of imagination with ideal elements in experience is generally recognized. Such is not the case with respect to its connection with faith. The latter has been regarded as a substitute for knowledge, for sight. It is defined, in the Christian religion, as *evidence* of things not seen. The implication is that faith is a kind of anticipatory vision of things that are now invisible because of the limitations of our finite and erring nature. Because it is a substitute for knowledge, its material and object are intellectual in quality. As John Locke summed up the matter, faith is "assent to a proposition . . . on the credit of its proposer." Religious faith is then given to a body of propositions as true on the credit of their supernatural author, reason coming in to demonstrate the reasonableness of giving such credit. Of necessity there results the development of theologies, or bodies of systematic propositions, to make explicit in organized form the content of the propositions to which belief is attached and assent given. Given the point of view, those who hold that religion necessarily implies a theology are correct.

But belief or faith has also a moral and practical import. Even devils, according to the older theologians, believe— and tremble. A distinction was made, therefore, between "speculative" or intellectual belief and an act called "justifying" faith. Apart from any theological context, there is a difference between belief that is a conviction that some end should be supreme over conduct, and belief that some object or being exists as a truth for the intellect. Conviction in the moral sense signifies being conquered, vanquished, in our active nature by an ideal end; it signifies acknowledgment of its rightful claim over our desires and purposes. Such acknowledgment is practical, not primarily intellectual. It goes beyond evidence that can be presented to *any* possible observer. Reflection, often long and arduous, may be involved in arriving at the conviction, but the import of thought is not exhausted in discovery of evidence that can justify intellectual assent. The authority of an ideal over choice and conduct is the authority of an ideal, not of a fact, of a truth guaranteed to intellect, not of the status of the one who propounds the truth.

Such moral faith is not easy. It was questioned of old whether the Son of Man should find faith on the earth in his coming. Moral faith has been bolstered by all sorts of arguments intended to prove that its object is not ideal and that its claim upon us is not primarily moral or practical, since the ideal in question is already embedded in the existent frame of things. It is argued that the ideal is already the final reality at the heart of things that exist, and that only our senses or the corruption of our natures prevent us from apprehending its prior existential being. Starting, say, from such an idea as that justice is more than a moral ideal because it is embedded in the very make-up of the actually existent world, men have gone on to build up vast intellectual schemes, philosophies, and theologies, to prove that ideals are real not as ideals but as antecedently existing actualities. They have failed to see that in converting moral realities into matters of intellectual assent they have evinced lack of *moral* faith. Faith that something should be in existence as far as lies in our power is changed into the intellectual belief that it is already in existence. When physical existence does not bear out the assertion, the physical is subtly changed into the metaphysical. In this way, moral faith has been inextricably tied up with intellectual beliefs about the supernatural.

The tendency to convert ends of moral faith and action into articles of an intellectual creed has been furthered by a tendency of which psychologists are well aware. What we ardently desire to have thus and so, we tend to believe is already so. Desire has a powerful influence upon intellectual beliefs. Moreover, when conditions are adverse to realization of the objects of our desire—and in the case of significant ideals they are extremely adverse—it is an easy way out to assume that after all they are already embodied in the ultimate structure of what is, and that appearances to the contrary are *merely* appearances. Imagination then merely supervenes and is freed from the responsibility for intervening. Weak natures take to reverie as a refuge as strong ones do to fanaticism. Those who dissent are mourned over by the first class and converted through the use of force by the second.

What has been said does not imply that all moral faith in ideal ends is by virtue of that fact religious in quality. The religious is "morality touched by emotion" only when the ends of moral conviction arouse emotions that are not only intense but are actuated and supported by ends so inclusive that they unify the self. The inclusiveness of the end in relation to both self and the "universe" to which an inclusive self is related is indispensable. According to the best authorities, "religion" comes from a root that means being bound or tied. Originally, it meant being bound by vows to a particular way of life—as les religieux were monks and nuns who had assumed certain vows. The religious attitude signifies something that is bound through imagination to a general attitude. This comprehensive attitude, moreover, is much broader than anything indicated by "moral" in its usual sense. The quality of attitude is displayed in art, science and good citizenship.

If we apply the conception set forth to the terms of the definition earlier quoted, these terms take on a new significance. An unseen power controlling our destiny becomes the power of an ideal. All possibilities, as possibilities, are ideal in character. The artist, scientist, citizen, parent, as far as they are actuated by the spirit of their callings, are controlled by the unseen. For all endeavor for the better is moved by faith in what is possible, not by adherence to the actual. Nor does this faith depend for its moving power upon intellectual assurance or belief that the things worked for must surely prevail and come into embodied existence. For the authority of the object to determine our attitude and conduct, the right that is given it to claim our allegiance and devotion is based on the intrinsic nature of the ideal. The outcome, given our best endeavor, is not with us. The inherent vice of all intellectual schemes of idealism is that they convert the idealism of action into a system of beliefs about antecedent reality. The character assigned this reality is so different from that which observation and reflection lead to and support that these schemes inevitably glide into alliance with the supernatural.

All religions, marked by elevated ideal quality, have dwelt upon the power of religion to introduce perspective into the piecemeal and shifting episodes of existence. Here too we need to reverse the ordinary statement and say that whatever introduces genuine perspective is religious, not that religion is something that introduces it. There can be no doubt (referring to the second element of the definition) of our dependence upon forces beyond our control. Primitive man was so impotent in the face of these forces that, especially in an unfavorable natural environment, fear became a dominant attitude, and, as the old saying goes, fear created the gods.

With increase of mechanisms of control, the element of fear has, relatively speaking, subsided. Some optimistic souls have even concluded that the forces about us are on the whole essentially benign. But every crisis, whether of the individual or of the community, reminds man of the precarious and partial nature of the control he exercises. When man, individually and collectively, has done his uttermost, conditions that at different times and places have given rise to the ideas of Fate and Fortune, of Chance and Providence, remain. It is the part of manliness to insist upon the capacity of mankind to strive to direct natural and social forces to humane ends. But unqualified absolutistic statements about the omnipotence of such endeavors reflect egoism rather than intelligent courage.

The fact that human destiny is so interwoven with forces beyond human control renders it unnecessary to suppose that dependence and the humility that accompanies it have to find the particular channel that is prescribed by traditional doctrines. What is especially significant is rather the form which the sense of dependence takes. Fear never gave stable perspective in the life of anyone. It is dispersive and withdrawing. Most religions have in fact added rites of communion to those of expiation and propitiation. For our dependence is manifested in those relations to the environment that support our undertakings and aspirations as much as it is in the defeats inflicted upon us. The essentially unreligious attitude is that which attributes human achievement and purpose to man in isolation from the world of physical nature and his fellows. Our successes are dependent upon the cooperation of nature. The sense of the dignity of human nature is as religious as is the sense of awe and reverence when it rests upon a sense of human nature as a coöperating part of a larger whole. Natural piety is not of necessity either a fatalistic acquiescence in natural happenings or a romantic idealization of the world. It may rest upon a just sense of nature as the whole of which we are parts, while it also recognizes that we are parts that are marked by intelligence and purpose, having the capacity to strive by their aid to bring conditions into greater consonance with what is humanly desirable. Such piety is an inherent constituent of a just perspective in life.

Understanding and knowledge also enter into a perspective that is religious in quality. Faith in the continued disclosing of truth through directed cooperative human endeavor is more religious in quality than is any faith in a completed revelation. It is of course now usual to hold that revelation is not completed in the sense of being ended. But religions hold that the essential framework is settled in its significant moral features at least, and that new elements that are offered must be judged by conformity to this framework. Some fixed doctrinal apparatus is necessary for *a* religion. But faith in the possibilities of continued and rigorous inquiry does not limit access to truth to any channel or scheme of things. It does not first say that truth is universal and then add there is but one road to it. It does not depend for assurance upon subjection to any dogma or item of doctrine. It trusts that the natural interactions between man and his environment will breed more intelligence and generate more knowledge provided the scientific methods that define intelligence in operation are pushed further into the mysteries of the world, being themselves promoted and improved in the operation. There is such a thing as faith in intelligence becoming religious in quality—a fact that perhaps explains the efforts of some religionists to disparage the possibilities of intelligence as a force. They properly feel such faith to be a dangerous rival.

Lives that are consciously inspired by loyalty to such

ideals as have been mentioned are still comparatively infrequent to the extent of that comprehensiveness and intensity which arouse an ardor religious in function. But before we infer the incompetency of such ideals and of the actions they inspire, we should at least ask ourselves how much of the existing situation is due to the fact that the religious factors of experience have been drafted into supernatural channels and thereby loaded with irrelevant encumbrances. A body of beliefs and practices that are apart from the common and natural relations of mankind must, in the degree in which it is influential, weaken and sap the force of the possibilities inherent in such relations. Here lies one aspect of the emancipation of the religious from religion.

Any activity pursued in behalf of an ideal end against obstacles and in spite of threats of personal loss because of conviction of its general and enduring value is religious in quality. Many a person, inquirer, artist, philanthropist, citizen, men and women in the humblest walks of life, have achieved, without presumption and without display, such unification of themselves and of their relations to the conditions of existence. It remains to extend their spirit and inspiration to ever wider numbers. If I have said anything about religions and religion that seems harsh, I have said those things because of a firm belief that the claim on the part of religions to possess a monopoly of ideals and of the supernatural means by which alone, it is alleged, they can be furthered, stands in the way of the realization of distinctively religious values inherent in natural experience. For that reason, if for no other, I should be sorry if any were misled by the frequency with which I have employed the adjective "religious" to conceive of what I have said as a disguised apology for what have passed as religions. The opposition between religious values as I conceive them and religions is not to be bridged. Just because the release of these values is so important, their identification with the creeds and cults of religions must be dissolved.

II

FAITH AND ITS OBJECT

All religions, as I pointed out in the preceding chapter, involve specific intellectual beliefs, and they attach—some greater, some less—importance to assent to these doctrines as true, true in the intellectual sense. They have literatures held especially sacred, containing historical material with which the validity of the religions is connected. They have developed a doctrinal apparatus it is incumbent upon "believers" (with varying degrees of strictness in different religions) to accept. They also insist that there is some special and isolated channel of access to the truths they hold.

No one will deny, I suppose, that the present crisis in religion is intimately bound up with these claims. The skepticism and agnosticism that are rife and that from the standpoint of the religionist are fatal to the religious spirit are directly bound up with the intellectual contents, historical, cosmological, ethical, and theological, asserted to be indispensable in everything religious. There is no need for me here to go with any minuteness into the causes that have generated doubt and disbelief, uncertainty and rejection, as to these contents. It is enough to point out that all the beliefs and ideas in question, whether having to do with historical and literary matters, or with astronomy, geology and biology, or with the creation and structure of the world and man, are connected with the supernatural, and that this connection is the factor that has brought doubt upon them; the factor that from the standpoint of historic and institutional religions is sapping the religious life itself.

The obvious and simple facts of the case are that some views about the origin and constitution of the world and man, some views about the course of human history and personages and incidents in that history, have become so interwoven with religion as to be identified with it. On the other hand, the growth of knowledge and of its methods and tests has been such as to make acceptance of these beliefs increasingly onerous and even impossible for large numbers of cultivated men and women. With such persons, the result is that the more these ideas are used as the basis and justification of a religion, the more dubious that religion becomes.

Protestant denominations have largely abandoned the idea that particular ecclesiastic sources can authoritatively determine cosmic, historic and theological beliefs. The more liberal among them have at least mitigated the older belief that individual hardness and corruption of heart are the causes of intellectual rejection of the intellectual apparatus of the Christian religion. But these denominations have also, with exceptions numerically insignificant, retained a certain indispensable minimum of intellectual content. They ascribe peculiar religious force to certain literary documents and certain historic personages. Even when they have greatly reduced the bulk of intellectual content to be accepted, they have insisted at least upon theism and the immortality of the individual.

It is no part of my intention to rehearse in any detail the weighty facts that collectively go by the name of the conflict of science and religion—a conflict that is not done away with by calling it a conflict of science with theology, as long as even a minimum of intellectual assent is prescribed as essential. The impact of astronomy not merely upon the older cosmogony of religion but upon elements of creeds dealing with historic events—witness the idea of ascent into heaven—is familiar. Geological discoveries have displaced creation myths which once bulked large. Biology has revolutionized conceptions of soul and mind which once occupied a central place in religious beliefs and ideas, and this science has made a profound impression upon ideas of sin, redemption, and immortality. Anthropology, history and literary criticism have furnished a radically different version of the historic events and personages upon which Christian religions have built. Psychology is already opening to us natural explanations of phenomena so extraordinary that once their supernatural origin was, so to say, the natural explanation.

The significant bearing for my purpose of all this is that new methods of inquiry and reflection have become for the educated man today the final arbiter of all questions of fact, existence, and intellectual assent. Nothing less than a revolution in the "seat of intellectual authority" has taken place. This revolution, rather than any particular aspect of its impact upon this and that religious belief, is the central thing. In this revolution, every defeat is a stimulus to renewed inquiry; every victory won is the open door to more discoveries, and every discovery is a new seed planted in the soil of intelligence, from which grow fresh plants with new fruits. The mind of man is being habituated to a new method and ideal: There is but one sure road of access to truth—the road of patient, coöperative inquiry operating by means of observation, experiment, record and controlled reflection.

The scope of the change is well illustrated by the fact that whenever a particular outpost is surrendered it is usually met by the remark from a liberal theologian that the particular doctrine or supposed historic or literary tenet surrendered was never, after all, an intrinsic part of religious belief, and that without it the true nature of religion stands out more clearly than before. Equally significant is the growing gulf between fundamentalists and liberals in the churches. What is not realized—although perhaps it is more definitely seen by fundamentalists than by liberals—is that the issue does not concern this and that piecemeal *item* of belief, but centers in the question of the method by which any and every item of intellectual belief is to be arrived at and justified.

The positive lesson is that religious qualities and values if they are real at all are not bound up with any single item of intellectual assent, not even that of the existence of the God of theism; and that, under existing conditions, the religious function in experience can be emancipated only through surrender of the whole notion of special truths that are religious by their own nature, together with the idea of peculiar avenues of access to such truths. For were we to admit that there is but one method for ascertaining fact and truth—that conveyed by the word "scientific" in its most general and generous sense—no discovery in any branch of knowledge and inquiry could then disturb the faith that is religious. I should describe this faith as the unification of the self through allegiance to inclusive ideal ends, which imagination presents to us and to which the human will responds as worthy of controlling our desires and choices.

It is probably impossible to imagine the amount of intellectual energy that has been diverted from normal processes of arriving at intellectual conclusions because it has gone into rationalization of the doctrines entertained by historic religions. The set that has thus been given the general mind is much more harmful, to my mind, than are the consequences of any one particular item of belief, serious as have been those flowing from acceptance of some of them. The modern liberal version of the intellectual content of Christianity seems to the modern mind to be more rational than some of the earlier doctrines that have been reacted against. Such is not the case in fact. The theological philosophers of the Middle Ages had no greater difficulty in giving rational form to all the doctrines of the Roman church than has the liberal theologian of today in formulating and justifying intellectually the doctrines he entertains. This statement is as applicable to the doctrine of continuing miracles, penance, indulgences, saints and angels, etc., as to the trinity, incarnation, atonement, and the sacraments. The fundamental question, I repeat, is not of this and that article of intellectual belief but of intellectual habit, method and criterion.

One method of swerving aside the impact of changed knowledge and method upon the intellectual content of religion is the method of division of territory and jurisdiction into two parts. Formerly these were called the realm of nature and the realm of grace. They are now often known as those of revelation and natural knowledge. Modern religious liberalism has no definite names for them, save, perhaps, the division, referred to in the last chapter, between scientific and religious experience. The implication is that in one territory the supremacy of scientific knowledge must be acknowledged, while there is another region, not very precisely defined, of intimate personal experience wherein other methods and criteria hold sway.

This method of justifying the peculiar and legitimate claim of certain elements of belief is always open to the objection that a positive conclusion is drawn from a negative fact. Existing ignorance or backwardness is employed to assert the existence of a division in the nature of the subject-matter dealt with. Yet the gap may only reflect, at most, a limitation now existing but in the future to be done away with. The argument that because some province or aspect of experience has not yet been "invaded" by scientific methods, it is not subject to them, is as old as it is dangerous. Time and time again, in some particular reserved field, it has been invalidated. Psychology is still in its infancy. He is bold to the point of rashness who asserts that intimate personal experience will never come within the ken of natural knowledge. It is more to the present point, however, to consider the region that is claimed by religionists as a special reserve. It is mystical experience. The difference, however, between mystic experience and the theory about it that is offered to us must be noted. The experience is a fact to be inquired into. The theory, like any theory, is an interpretation of the fact. The idea that by its very nature the experience is a veridical realization of the direct presence of God does not rest so much upon examination of the facts as it does upon importing into their interpretation a conception that is formed outside them. In its dependence upon a prior conception of the supernatural, which is the thing to be proved, it begs the question.

History exhibits many types of mystic experience, and each of these types is contemporaneously explained by the concepts that prevail in the culture and the circle in which the phenomena occur. There are mystic crises that arise, as among some North American Indian tribes, induced by fasting. They are accompanied by trances and semi-hysteria. Their purpose is to gain some special power, such perhaps as locating a person who is lost or finding objects that have been secreted. There is the mysticism of Hindoo practice now enjoying some vogue in Western countries. There is the mystic ecstasy of Neoplatonism with its complete abrogation of the self and absorption into an impersonal whole of Being. There is the mysticism of intense æsthetic experience independent of any theological or metaphysical interpretation. There is the heretical mysticism of William Blake. There is the mysticism of sudden unreasoning fear in which the very foundations seem shaken beneath one—to mention but a few of the types that may be found.

What common element is there between, say, the Neoplatonic conception of a super-divine Being wholly apart from human needs and conditions and the medieval theory of an immediate union that is fostered through attention to the sacraments or through concentration upon the heart of Jesus? The contemporary emphasis of some Protestant theologians upon the sense of inner personal communion with God, found in religious experience, is almost as far away from medieval Christianity as it is from Neoplatonism or Yoga. Interpretations of the experience have not grown from the experience itself with the aid of such scientific resources as may be available. They have been imported by borrowing without criticism from ideas that are current in the surrounding culture.

The mystic states of the shaman and of some North American Indians are frankly techniques for gaining a special power—*the* power as it is conceived by some revivalist sects. There is no especial intellectual objectification accompanying the experience. The knowledge that is said to be gained is not that of Being but of particular secrets and occult modes of operation. The aim is not to gain knowledge of superior divine power, but to get advice, cures for the sick, prestige, etc. The conception that mystic experience is a normal mode of religious experience by which we may acquire knowledge of God and divine things is a nineteenth-century interpretation that has gained vogue in direct ratio to the decline of older methods of religious apologetics.

There is no reason for denying the existence of experiences that are called mystical. On the contrary, there is every reason to suppose that, in some degree of intensity, they occur so frequently that they may be regarded as normal manifestations that take place at certain rhythmic points in the movement of experience. The assumption that denial of a particular interpretation of their objective content proves that those who make the denial do not have the experience in question, so that if they had it they would be equally persuaded of its objective source in the presence of God, has no foundation in fact. As with every empirical phenomenon, the occurrence of the state called mystical is simply an occasion for inquiry into its mode of causation. There is no more reason for converting the experience itself into an immediate knowledge of its cause than in the case of an experience of lightning or any other natural occurrence.

My purpose, then, in this brief reference to mysticism is not to throw doubt upon the existence of particular experiences called mystical. Nor is it to propound any theory to account for them. I have referred to the matter merely as an illustration of the general tendency to mark off two distinct realms in one of which science has jurisdiction, while in the other, special modes of immediate knowledge of religious objects have authority. This dualism as it operates in contemporary interpretation of mystic experience in order to validate certain beliefs is but a reinstatement of the old dualism between the natural and the supernatural, in terms better adapted to the cultural conditions of the present time. Since it is the conception of the supernatural that science calls in question, the circular nature of this type of reasoning is obvious.

Apologists for a religion often point to the shift that goes on in scientific ideas and materials as evidence of the unreliability of science as a mode of knowledge. They often seem peculiarly elated by the great, almost revolutionary, change in fundamental physical conceptions that has taken place in science during the present generation. Even if the alleged unreliability were as great as they assume (or even greater), the question would remain: Have we any other recourse for knowledge? But in fact they miss the point. Science is not constituted by any particular body of subject-matter. It is constituted by a method, a method of changing beliefs by means of tested inquiry as well as of arriving at them. It is its glory, not its condemnation, that its subject-matter develops as the method is improved. There is no special subject-matter of belief that is sacrosanct. The identification of science with a particular set of beliefs and ideas is itself a holdover of ancient and still current dogmatic habits of thought which are opposed to science in its actuality and which science is undermining.

For scientific method is adverse not only to dogma but to doctrine as well, provided we take "doctrine" in its usual meaning—a body of definite beliefs that need only to be taught and learned as true. This negative attitude of science to doctrine does not indicate indifference to truth. It signifies supreme loyalty to the method by which truth is attained. The scientific-religious conflict ultimately is a conflict between allegiance to this method and allegiance to even an irreducible minimum of belief so fixed in advance that it can never be modified.

The method of intelligence is open and public. The doctrinal method is limited and private. This limitation persists even when knowledge of the truth that is religious is said to be arrived at by a special mode of experience, that termed "religious." For the latter is assumed to be a very special kind of experience. To be sure it is asserted to be open to all who obey certain conditions. Yet the mystic experience yields, as we have seen, various results in the way of belief to different persons, depending upon the surrounding culture of those who undergo it. As a method, it lacks the public character belonging to the method of intelligence. Moreover, when the experience in question does not yield consciousness of the presence of God, in the sense that is alleged to exist, the retort is always at hand that it is not a genuine religious experience. For by definition, only that experience *is* religious which arrives at this particular result. The argument is circular. The traditional position is that some hardness or corruption of heart prevents one from having the experience. Liberal religionists are now more humane. But their logic does not differ.

It is sometimes held that beliefs about religious matters are symbolic, like rites and ceremonies. This view may be an advance upon that which holds to their literal objective validity. But as usually put forward it suffers from an ambiguity. Of what are the beliefs symbols? Are they symbols of things experienced in other modes than those set apart as religious, so that the things symbolized have an independent standing? Or are they symbols in the sense of standing for some transcendental reality—transcendental because not being the subject-matter of experience generally? Even the fundamentalist admits a certain quality and degree of symbolism in the latter sense in objects of religious belief. For he holds that the objects of these beliefs are so far beyond finite human capacity that our beliefs must be couched in more or less metaphorical terms. The conception that faith is the best available substitute for knowledge in our present estate still attaches to the notion of the symbolic character of the materials of faith; unless by ascribing to them a symbolic nature we mean that these materials stand for something that is verifiable in general and public experience.

Were we to adopt the latter point of view, it would be evident not only that the intellectual articles of a creed must be understood to be symbolic of moral and other ideal values, but that the facts taken to be historic and used as concrete evidence of the intellectual articles are themselves symbolic. These articles of a creed present events and persons that have been made over by the idealizing imagination in the interest, at their best, of moral ideals. Historic personages in their divine attributes are materializations of the ends that enlist devotion and inspire endeavor. They are symbolic of the reality of ends moving us in many forms of experience. The ideal values that are thus symbolized also mark human experience in science and art and the various modes of human association: they mark almost everything in life that rises from the level of manipulation of conditions as they exist. It is admitted that the objects of religion are ideal in contrast with our present state. What would be lost if it were also admitted that they have authoritative claim upon conduct just because they are ideal? The assumption that these objects of religion exist already in some realm of Being seems to add nothing to their force, while it weakens their claim over us as ideals, in so far as it bases that claim upon matters that are intellectually dubious. The question narrows itself to this: Are the ideals that move us genuinely ideal or are they ideal only in contrast with our present estate?

The import of the question extends far. It determines the meaning given to the word "God." On one score, the word can mean only a particular Being. On the other score, it denotes the unity of all ideal ends arousing us to desire and actions. Does the unification have a claim upon our attitude and conduct because it is already, apart from us, in realized existence, or because of its own inherent meaning and value? Suppose for the moment that the word "God" means the ideal ends that at a given time and place one acknowledges as having authority over his volition and emotion, the values to which one is supremely devoted, as far as these ends, through imagination, take on unity. If we make this supposition, the issue will stand out clearly in contrast with the doctrine of religions that "God" designates some kind of Being having prior and therefore non-ideal existence.

The word "non-ideal" is to be taken literally in regard to some religions that have historically existed, to all of them as far as they are neglectful of moral qualities in their divine beings. It does not apply in the same *literal* way to Judaism and Christianity. For they have asserted that the Supreme Being has moral and spiritual attributes. But it applies to them none the less in that these moral and spiritual characters are thought of as properties of a particular existence and are thought to be of religious value for us because of this embodiment in such an existence. Here, as far as I can see, is the ultimate issue as to the difference between *a* religion and the religious as a function of experience.

The idea that "God" represents a unification of ideal values that is essentially imaginative in origin when the imagination supervenes in conduct is attended with verbal difficulties owing to our frequent use of the word "imagination" to denote fantasy and doubtful reality. But the reality of ideal ends as ideals is vouched for by their undeniable power in action. An ideal is not an illusion because imagination is the organ through which it is apprehended. For *all* possibilities reach us through the imagination. In a definite sense the only meaning that can be assigned the term "imagination" is that things unrealized in fact come home to us and have power to stir us. The unification effected through imagination is not fanciful, for it is the reflex of the unification of practical and emotional attitudes. The unity signifies not a single Being, but the unity of loyalty and effort evoked by the fact that many ends are one in the power of their ideal, or imaginative, quality to stir and hold us.

We may well ask whether the power and significance in life of the traditional conceptions of God are not due to the ideal qualities referred to by them, the hypostatization of them into an existence being due to a conflux of tendencies in human nature that converts the object of desire into an antecedent reality (as was mentioned in the previous chapter) with beliefs that have prevailed in the cultures of the past. For in the older cultures the idea of the supernatural was "natural," in the sense in which "natural" signifies something customary and familiar. It seems more credible that religious persons have been supported and consoled by the reality with which ideal values appeal to them than that they have been upborne by sheer matter of fact existence. That, when once men are inured to the idea of the union of the ideal and the physical, the two should be so bound together in emotion that it is difficult to institute a separation, agrees with all we know of human psychology.

The benefits that will accrue, however, from making the separation are evident. The dislocation frees the religious values of experience once for all from matters that are continually becoming more dubious. With that release there comes emancipation from the necessity of resort to apologetics. The reality of ideal ends and values in their authority over us is an undoubted fact. The validity of justice, affection, and that intellectual correspondence of our ideas with realities that we call truth, is so assured in its hold upon humanity that it is unnecessary for the religious attitude to encumber itself with the apparatus of dogma and doctrine. Any other conception of the religious attitude, when it is adequately analyzed, means that those who hold it care more for force than for ideal values—since all that an Existence can add is force to establish, to punish, and to reward. There are, indeed, some persons who frankly say that their own faith does not require any guarantee that moral values are backed up by physical force, but who hold that the masses are so backward that ideal values will not affect their conduct unless in the popular belief these values have the sanction of a power that can enforce them and can execute justice upon those who fail to comply.

There are some persons, deserving of more respect, who

say: "We agree that the beginning must be made with the primacy of the ideal. But why stop at this point? Why not search with the utmost eagerness and vigor for all the evidence we can find, such as is supplied by history, by presence of design in nature, which may lead on to the belief that the ideal is already extant in a Personality having objective existence?"

One answer to the question is that we are involved by this search in all the problems of the existence of evil that have haunted theology in the past and that the most ingenious apologetics have not faced, much less met. If these apologists had not identified the existence of ideal goods with that of a Person supposed to originate and support them—a Being, moreover, to whom omnipotent power is attributed —the problem of the occurrence of evil would be gratuitous. The significance of ideal ends and meanings is, indeed, closely connected with the fact that there are in life all sorts of things that are evil to us because we would have them otherwise. Were existing conditions wholly good, the notion of possibilities to be realized would never emerge.

But the more basic answer is that while if the search is conducted upon a strictly empirical basis there is no reason why it should not take place, as a matter of fact it is always undertaken in the interest of the supernatural. Thus it diverts attention and energy from ideal values and from the exploration of actual conditions by means of which they may be promoted. History is testimony to this fact. Men have never fully used the powers they possess to advance the good in life, because they have waited upon some power external to themselves and to nature to do the work they are responsible for doing. Dependence upon an external power is the counterpart of surrender of human endeavor. Nor is emphasis on exercising our own powers for good an egoistical or a sentimentally optimistic recourse. It is not the first, for it does not isolate man, either individually or collectively, from nature. It is not the second, because it makes no assumption beyond that of the need and responsibility for human endeavor, and beyond the conviction that, if human desire and endeavor were enlisted in behalf of natural ends, conditions would be bettered. It involves no expectation of a millennium of good.

Belief in the supernatural as a necessary power for apprehension of the ideal and for practical attachment to it has for its counterpart a pessimistic belief in the corruption and impotency of natural means. That is axiomatic in Christian dogma. But this apparent pessimism has a way of suddenly changing into an exaggerated optimism. For according to the terms of the doctrine, if the faith in the supernatural is of the required order, regeneration at once takes place. Goodness, in all essentials, is thereby established; if not, there is proof that the established relation to the supernatural has been vitiated. This romantic optimism is one cause for the excessive attention to individual salvation characteristic of traditional Christianity. Belief in a sudden and complete transmutation through conversion and in the objective efficacy of prayer, is too easy a way out of difficulties. It leaves matters in general just about as they were before; that is, sufficiently bad so that there is additional support for the idea that only supernatural aid can better them. The position of natural intelligence is that there exists a *mixture* of good and evil, and that reconstruction in the direction of the good which is indicated by ideal ends, must take place, if at all, through continued cooperative effort. There is at least enough impulse toward justice, kindliness, and order so that if it were mobilized for action, not expecting abrupt and complete transformation to occur, the disorder, cruelty, and oppression that exist would be reduced.

The discussion has arrived at a point where a more fundamental objection to the position I am taking needs consideration. The misunderstanding upon which this objection rests should be pointed out. The view I have advanced is sometimes treated as if the identification of the divine with ideal ends left the ideal wholly without roots in existence and without support from existence. The objection implies that my view commits one to such a separation of the ideal and the existent that the ideal has no chance to find lodgment even as a seed that might grow and bear fruit. On the contrary, what I have been criticizing is the *identification* of the ideal with a particular Being, especially when that identification makes necessary the conclusion that this Being is outside of nature, and what I have tried to show is that the ideal itself has its roots in natural conditions; it emerges when the imagination idealizes existence by laying hold of the possibilities offered to thought and action. There are values, goods, actually realized upon a natural basis—the goods of human association, of art and knowledge. The idealizing imagination seizes upon the most precious things found in the climacteric moments of experience and projects them. We need no external criterion and guarantee for their goodness. They are had, they exist as good, and out of them we frame our ideal ends.

Moreover, the ends that result from our projection of experienced goods into objects of thought, desire and effort exist, only they exist *as* ends. Ends, purposes, exercise determining power in human conduct. The aims of philanthropists, of Florence Nightingale, of Howard, of Wilberforce, of Peabody, have not been idle dreams. They have modified institutions. Aims, ideals, do not exist simply in "mind"; they exist in character, in personality and action. One might call the roll of artists, intellectual inquirers, parents, friends, citizens who are neighbors, to show that purposes exist in an *operative* way. What I have been objecting to, I repeat, is not the idea that ideals are linked with existence and that they themselves exist, through human embodiment, as forces, but the idea that their authority and value depend upon some prior complete embodiment—as if the efforts of human beings in behalf of justice, or knowledge or beauty, depended for their effectiveness and validity upon assurance that there already existed in some supernal region a place where criminals are humanely treated, where there is no serfdom or slavery, where all facts and truths are already discovered and possessed, and all beauty is eternally displayed in actualized form.

The aims and ideals that move us are generated through imagination. But they are not made out of imaginary stuff. They are made out of the hard stuff of the world of physical and social experience. The locomotive did not exist before Stevenson, nor the telegraph before the time of Morse. But

imagination
not faith

45

the conditions for their existence were there in physical material and energies and in human capacity. Imagination seized hold upon the idea of a rearrangement of existing things that would evolve new objects. The same thing is true of a painter, a musician, a poet, a philanthropist, a moral prophet. The new vision does not arise out of nothing, but emerges through seeing, in terms of possibilities, that is, of imagination, old things in new relations serving a new end which the new end aids in creating.

Moreover the process of creation is experimental and continuous. The artist, scientific man, or good citizen, depends upon what others have done before him and are doing around him. The sense of new values that become ends to be realized arises first in dim and uncertain form. As the values are dwelt upon and carried forward in action they grow in definiteness and coherence. Interaction between aim and existent conditions improves and tests the ideal; and conditions are at the same time modified. Ideals change as they are applied in existent conditions. The process endures and advances with the life of humanity. What one person and one group accomplish becomes the standing ground and starting point of those who succeed them. When the vital factors in this natural process are generally acknowledged in emotion, thought and action, the process will be both accelerated and purified through elimination of that irrelevant element that culminates in the idea of the supernatural. When the vital factors attain the religious force that has been drafted into supernatural religions, the resulting reinforcement will be incalculable.

These considerations may be applied to the idea of God,

or, to avoid misleading conceptions, to the idea of the divine. This idea is, as I have said, one of ideal possibilities unified through imaginative realization and projection. But this idea of God, or of the divine, is also connected with all the natural forces and conditions—including man and human association—that promote the growth of the ideal and that further its realization. We are in the presence neither of ideals completely embodied in existence nor yet of ideals that are mere rootless ideals, fantasies, utopias. For there are forces in nature and society that generate and support the ideals. They are further unified by the action that gives them coherence and solidity. It is this *active* relation between ideal and actual to which I would give the name "God." I would not insist that the name *must* be given. There are those who hold that the associations of the term with the supernatural are so numerous and close that any use of the word "God" is sure to give rise to misconception and be taken as a concession to traditional ideas.

They may be correct in this view. But the facts to which I have referred are there, and they need to be brought out with all possible clearness and force. There exist concretely and experimentally goods—the values of art in all its forms, of knowledge, of effort and of rest after striving, of education and fellowship, of friendship and love, of growth in mind and body. These goods are there and yet they are relatively embryonic. Many persons are shut out from generous participation in them; there are forces at work that threaten and sap existent goods as well as prevent their expansion. A clear and intense conception of a union of ideal ends with actual conditions is capable of arousing steady emotion. It may be fed by every experience, no matter what its material.

In a distracted age, the need for such an idea is urgent. It can unify interests and energies now dispersed; it can direct action and generate the heat of emotion and the light of intelligence. Whether one gives the name "God" to this union, operative in thought and action, is a matter for individual decision. But the *function* of such a working union of the ideal and actual seems to me to be identical with the force that has in fact been attached to the conception of God in all the religions that have a spiritual content; and a clear idea of that function seems to me urgently needed at the present time.

The sense of this union may, with some persons, be furthered by mystical experiences, using the term "mystical" in its broadest sense. That result depends largely upon temperament. But there is a marked difference between the union associated with mysticism and the union which I had in mind. There is nothing mystical about the latter; it is natural and moral. Nor is there anything mystical about the perception or consciousness of such union. Imagination of ideal ends pertinent to actual conditions represents the fruition of a disciplined mind. There is, indeed, even danger that resort to mystical experiences will be an escape, and that its result will be the passive feeling that the union of actual and ideal is already accomplished. But in fact this union is active and practical; it is a *uniting*, not something given.

One reason why personally I think it fitting to use the word "God" to denote that uniting of the ideal and actual which has been spoken of, lies in the fact that aggressive atheism seems to me to have something in common with traditional supernaturalism. I do not mean merely that the former is mainly so negative that it fails to give positive direction to thought, though that fact is pertinent. What I have in mind especially is the exclusive preoccupation of both militant atheism and supernaturalism with man in isolation. For in spite of supernaturalism's reference to something beyond nature, it conceives of this earth as the moral center of the universe and of man as the apex of the whole scheme of things. It regards the drama of sin and redemption enacted within the isolated and lonely soul of man as the one thing of ultimate importance. Apart from man, nature is held either accursed or negligible. Militant atheism is also affected by lack of natural piety. The ties binding man to nature that poets have always celebrated are passed over lightly. The attitude taken is often that of man living in an indifferent and hostile world and issuing blasts of defiance. A religious attitude, however, needs the sense of a connection of man, in the way of both dependence and support, with the enveloping world that the imagination feels is a universe. Use of the words "God" or "divine" to convey the union of actual with ideal may protect man from a sense of isolation and from consequent despair or defiance.

In any case, whatever the name, the meaning is selective. For it involves no miscellaneous worship of everything in general. It selects those factors in existence that generate and support our idea of good as an end to be striven for. It excludes a multitude of forces that at any given time are irrelevant to this function. Nature produces whatever gives reinforcement and direction but also what occasions discord and confusion. The "divine" is thus a term of human choice and aspiration. A humanistic religion, if it excludes our relation to nature, is pale and thin, as it is presumptuous, when it takes humanity as an object of worship. Matthew Arnold's conception of a "power not ourselves" is too narrow in its reference to operative and sustaining conditions. While it is selective, it is too narrow in its basis of selection—righteousness. The conception thus needs to be widened in two ways. The powers that generate and support the good as experienced and as ideal, work *within* as well as without. There seems to be a reminiscence of an external Jehovah in Arnold's statement. And the powers work to enforce other values and ideals than righteousness. Arnold's sense of an opposition between Hellenism and Hebraism resulted in exclusion of beauty, truth, and friendship from the list of the consequences toward which powers work within and without.

In the relation between nature and human ends and endeavors, recent science has broken down the older dualism. It has been engaged in this task for three centuries. But as long as the conceptions of science were strictly mechanical (mechanical in the sense of assuming separate things acting upon one another purely externally by push and pull), religious apologists had a standing ground in pointing out the differences between man and physical nature. The differences could be used for arguing that something supernatural had intervened in the case of man. The recent acclaim, however, by apologists for religion of the surrender by science of the classic type of mechanicalism* seems ill-advised from their own point of view. For the change in the modern scientific view of nature simply brings man and nature nearer together. We are no longer compelled to choose between explaining away what is distinctive in man through reducing him to another form of a mechanical model and the doctrine that something literally supernatural marks him off from nature. The less mechanical—in its older sense—physical nature is found to be, the closer is man to nature.

In his fascinating book, *The Dawn of Conscience*, James Henry Breasted refers to Haeckel as saying that the question he would most wish to have answered is this: Is the universe friendly to man? The question is an ambiguous one. Friendly to man in what respect? With respect to ease and comfort, to material success, to egoistic ambitions? Or to his aspiration to inquire and discover, to invent and create, to build a more secure order for human existence? In whatever form the question be put, the answer cannot in all honesty be an unqualified and absolute one. Mr. Breasted's answer, as a historian, is that nature has been friendly to the emergence and development of conscience and character. Those who will have all or nothing cannot be satisfied with this answer. Emergence and growth are not enough for them. They want something more than growth accompanied by toil and pain. They want final achievement. Others who are less absolutist may be content to think that, morally speaking, growth is a

---

*I use this term because science has not abandoned its beliefs in working mechanisms in giving up the idea that they are of the nature of a strictly mechanical contact of discrete things.

higher value and ideal than is sheer attainment. They will remember also that growth has not been confined to conscience and character; that it extends also to discovery, learning and knowledge, to creation in the arts, to furtherance of ties that hold men together in mutual aid and affection. These persons at least will be satisfied with an intellectual view of the religious function that is based on continuing choice directed toward ideal ends.

For, I would remind readers in conclusion, it is the intellectual side of the religious attitude that I have been considering. I have suggested that the religious element in life has been hampered by conceptions of the supernatural that were imbedded in those cultures wherein man had little control over outer nature and little in the way of sure method of inquiry and test. The crisis today as to the intellectual content of religious belief has been caused by the change in the intellectual climate due to the increase of our knowledge and our means of understanding. I have tried to show that this change is not fatal to the religious values in our common experience, however adverse its impact may be upon historic religions. Rather, provided that the methods and results of intelligence at work are frankly adopted, the change is liberating.

It clarifies our ideals, rendering them less subject to illusion and fantasy. It relieves us of the incubus of thinking of them as fixed, as without power of growth. It discloses that they develop in coherence and pertinency with increase of natural intelligence. The change gives aspiration for natural knowledge a definitely religious character, since growth in understanding of nature is seen to be organically related to the formation of ideal ends. The same change enables man to select those elements in natural conditions that may be organized to support and extend the sway of ideals. All purpose is selective, and all intelligent action includes deliberate choice. In the degree in which we cease to depend upon belief in the supernatural, selection is enlightened and choice can be made in behalf of ideals whose inherent relations to conditions and consequences are understood. Were the naturalistic foundations and bearings of religion grasped, the religious element in life would emerge from the throes of the crisis in religion. Religion would then be found to have its natural place in every aspect of human experience that is concerned with estimate of possibilities, with emotional stir by possibilities as yet unrealized, and with all action in behalf of their realization. All that is significant in human experience falls within this frame.

III

THE HUMAN ABODE
OF THE RELIGIOUS FUNCTION

In discussing the intellectual content of religion before considering religion in its social connections, I did not follow the usual temporal order. Upon the whole, collective modes of practice either come first or are of greater importance. The core of religions has generally been found in rites and ceremonies. Legends and myths grow up in part as decorative dressings, in response to the irrepressible human tendency toward story-telling, and in part as attempts to explain ritual practices. Then as culture advances, stories are consolidated, and theogonies and cosmogonies are formed—as with the Babylonians, Egyptians, Hebrews and Greeks. In the case of the Greeks, the stories of creation and accounts of the constitution of the world were mainly poetic and literary, and philosophies ultimately developed from them. In most cases, legends along with rites and ceremonies came under the guardianship of a special body, the priesthood, and were subject to the special arts which it possessed. A special group was set aside as the responsible owners, protectors, and promulgators of the corpus of beliefs.

But the formation of a special social group having a peculiar relation to both the practices and the beliefs of religion is but part of the story. In the widest perspective, it is the less important part. The more significant point as regards the social import of religion is that the priesthoods were official representatives of some community, tribe, city-state or empire. Whether there was a priesthood or not, individuals who were members of a community were born into a religious community as they were into social and political organization. Each social group had its own divine beings who were its founders and protectors. Its rites of sacrifice, purification, and communion were manifestations of organized civic life. The temple was a public institution, the focus of the worship of the community; the influence of its practices extended to all the customs of the community, domestic, economic, and political. Even wars between groups were usually conflicts of their respective deities.

An individual did not join a church. He was born and reared in a community whose social unity, organization and traditions were symbolized and celebrated in the rites, cults and beliefs of a collective religion. Education was the induction of the young into community activities that were interwoven at every point with customs, legends and ceremonies intimately connected with and sanctioned by a religion. There are a few persons, especially those brought up in Jewish communities in Russia, who can understand without the use of imagination what a religion means socially when it permeates all the customs and activities of group life. To most of us in the United States such a situation is only a remote historic episode.

The change that has taken place in conditions once universal and now infrequent is in my opinion the greatest change that has occurred in religion in all history. The intellectual conflict of scientific and theological beliefs has attracted much more attention. It is still near the focus of attention. But the change in the social center of gravity of religion has gone on so steadily and is now so generally accomplished that it has faded from the thought of most persons, save perhaps the historians, and even they are especially aware of it only in its political aspect. For the conflict between state and church still continues in some countries.

There are even now persons who are born into a particular church, that of their parents, and who take membership in it almost as a matter of course; indeed, the fact of such membership may be an important, even a determining, factor in an individual's whole career. But the thing new in history, the thing once unheard of, is that the organization in question is a *special* institution within a secular community. Even where there are established churches, they are constituted by the state and may be unmade by the state. Not only the national state but other forms of organization among groups have grown in power and influence at the expense of organizations built upon and about a religion. The correlate of this fact is that membership in associations of the latter type is more and more a matter of the voluntary choice of individuals, who may tend to accept responsibilities imposed by the church but who accept them of their own volition. If they do accept them, the organization they join is, in many nations, chartered under a general corporation law of the political and secular entity.

The shift in what I have called the social center of gravity accompanies the enormous expansion of associations formed for educational, political, economic, philanthropic and scientific purposes, which has occurred independently of any religion. These social modes have grown so much that they exercise the greater hold upon the thought and interest of most persons, even of those holding membership in churches. This positive extension of interests which, from the standpoint of a religion, are non-religious, is so great that in comparison with it the direct effect of science upon the creeds of religion seems to me of secondary importance.

I say, the *direct* effect; for the indirect effect of science in stimulating the growth of competing organizations is enormous. Changes that are purely intellectual affect at most but a small number of specialists. They are secondary to consequences brought about through impact upon the *conditions* under which human beings associate with one another. Invention and technology, in alliance with industry and commerce, have, needless to say, profoundly affected these underlying conditions of association. Every political and social problem of the present day reflects this indirect influence, from unemployment to banking, from municipal administration to the great migration of peoples made possible by new modes of transportation, from birth control to foreign commerce and war. The social changes that have come about through application of the new knowledge affect everyone, whether he is aware or not of the source of the play upon him. The effect is the deeper, indeed largely unconscious. For, to repeat what I have ~ ditions under which people meet and act togetl modified.

The fundamentalist in religion is one whose beliefs in intellectual content have hardly been touched by scientific developments. His notions about heaven and earth and man, as far as their bearing on religion is concerned, are hardly more affected by the work of Copernicus, Newton, and Darwin than they are by that of Einstein. But his actual life, in what he does day by day and in the contacts that are set up, has been radically changed by political and economic changes that have followed from applications of science. As far as strictly intellectual changes are concerned, creeds display great power of accommodation; their articles undergo insensible change of perspective; emphases are altered, and new meanings creep in. The Catholic Church, particularly, has shown leniency in dealing with intellectual deviations as long as they do not touch discipline, rites, and sacraments.

Among the laity only a small number, the more highly educated section, is directly affected by changes in scientific beliefs. Certain ideas recede more or less into the background but are not seriously challenged; nominally they are accepted. Probably most educated people thought the conception of biological evolution had been accepted as a commonplace until legislation in Tennessee and the Scopes trial brought about an acute crisis that revealed how far that was from being the case. Within an ecclesiastic organization, on the other hand, the class of professionals does not sense the change in perspective and emphasis of values in the general mind until some acute situation reveals it. Then they vigorously deny the validity of the new interests that have arisen. But since they are working against interests rather than merely against ideas, their desperate efforts are not convincing except for those already convinced.

Changes in practice that affect collective life go deep and extend far. They have been operating ever since the time we call the Middle Ages. The Renaissance was essentially a new birth of secularism. The development of the idea of "natural religion," characteristic of the eighteenth century, was a protest against control by ecclesiastic bodies—a movement foreshadowed in this respect by the growth of "independent" religious societies in the preceding century. But natural religion no more denied the intellectual validity of supernatural ideas than did the growth of independent congregations. It attempted rather to justify theism and immortality on the basis of the natural reason of the individual. The transcendentalism of the nineteenth century was a further move in the same general direction, a movement in which "reason" took on a more romantic, more colorful, and more collective form. It asserted the diffusion of the supernatural through secular life.

These movements and others not mentioned are the intellectual reflex of the greatest revolution that has taken place in religions during the thousands of years that man has been upon earth. For, as I have said, this change has to do with the *social* place and function of religion. Even the hold of the supernatural upon the general mind has become more and more disassociated from the power of ecclesiastic organization—that is, of any particular form of communal organization. Thus the very idea that was central in religions has more and more oozed away, so to speak, from the guardianship and care of any particular social institution. Even more important is the fact that a steady encroachment upon ecclesiastic institutions of forms of association once regarded as secular has altered the way in which men spend their time in work, recreation, citizenship, and political action. The essential point is not just that secular organizations and actions are legally or externally severed from the control of the church, but that interests and values unrelated to the offices of any church now so largely sway the desires and aims of even believers.

The individual believer may indeed carry the disposition and motivation he has acquired through affiliation with a religious organization into his political action, into his connection with schools, even into his business and amusements. But there remain two facts that constitute a revolution. In the first place, conditions are such that this action is a matter of personal choice and resolution on the part of individuals, not of the very nature of social organization. In the second place, the very fact that an individual imports or carries his personal attitude into affairs that are inherently secular, that are outside the scope of religion, constitutes an enormous change, in spite of the belief that secular matters *should* be permeated by the spirit of religion. Even if it be asserted, as it is by some religionists, that all the new movements and interests of any value grew up under the auspices of a church and received their impetus from the same source, it must be admitted that once the vessels have been launched, they are sailing on strange seas to far lands. Here, it seems to me, is the issue to be faced. Here is the place where the distinction that I have drawn between a religion and the religious function is peculiarly applicable. It is of the nature of a religion based on the supernatural to draw a line between the religious and the secular and profane, even when it asserts the rightful authority of the Church and its religion to dominate these other interests. The conception that "religious" signifies a certain attitude and outlook, independent of the supernatural, necessitates no such division. It does not shut religious values up within a particular compartment, nor assume that a particular form of association bears a unique relation to it. Upon the social side the future of the religious function seems preëminently bound up with its emancipation from religions and a particular religion. Many persons feel perplexed because of the multiplicity of churches and the conflict of their claims. But the fundamental difficulty goes deeper.

In what has been said I have not ignored the interpretation put, by representatives of religious organizations, upon the historic change that has occurred. The oldest organization, the Roman Catholic church, judges the secularization of life, the growing independence of social interests and values from control by the church, as but one evidence the more of the apostasy of the natural man from God: the corruption inherent in the will of mankind has resulted in defiance of the authority that God has delegated to his designated representatives on earth. This church points to the fact that secularization has proceeded *pari passu* with the extension of Protestantism as evidence of the wilful heresy of the latter in its appeal to private conscience and choice. The remedy is simple. Submission to the will of God, as continuously expressed through the organization that is his established vicegerent on earth, is the sole means by which social relations and values can again become coextensive with religion.

Protestant churches, on the contrary, have emphasized the fact that the relation of man to God is primarily an individual matter, a matter of personal choice and responsibility. From this point of view, one aspect of the change outlined marks an advance that is religious as well as moral. For according to it, the beliefs and rites that tend to make relation of man to God a collective and institutional affair erect barriers between the human soul and the divine spirit. Communion with God must be initiated by the individual's heart and will through direct divine assistance. Hence the change that has occurred in the social status of organized religion is nothing to deplore. What has been lost was at best specious and external. What has been gained is that religion has been placed upon its only real and solid foundation: direct relationship of conscience and will to God. Although there is much that is non-Christian and anti-Christian in existing economic and political institutions, it is better that change be accomplished by the sum total of efforts of men and women who are imbued with personal faith, than that they be effected by any wholesale institutional effort that subordinates the individual to an external and ultimately a worldly authority.

Were the question involved in these two opposed views taken up in detail, there are some specific considerations that might be urged. It might be urged that the progressive secularization of the interests of life has not been attended by the increasing degeneration that the argument of the first group implies. There are many who, as historical students, independent of affiliation with any religion, would regard reversal of the process of secularization and return to conditions in which the Church was the final authority as a menace to things held most precious. With reference to the position of Protestantism, it may be urged that in fact such social advances as have taken place are not the product of voluntary religious associations; that, on the contrary, the forces that have worked to humanize human relations, that have resulted in intellectual and æsthetic development, have come from influences that are independent of the churches. A case could be made out for the position that the churches have lagged behind in most important social movements and that they have turned their chief attention in social affairs to moral *symptoms*, to vices and abuses, like drunkenness, sale of intoxicants, divorce, rather than to the causes of war and of the long list of economic and political injustices and oppressions. Protest against the latter has been mainly left to secular movements.

In earlier times, what we now call the supernatural hardly meant anything more definite than the extraordinary, that which was striking and emotionally impressive because of its out-of-the-way character. Probably even today the commonest conception of the natural is that which is usual, customary and familiar. When there is no insight into the cause of unusual events, belief in the supernatural is itself "natural"—in this sense of natural. Supernaturalism was, therefore, a genuinely social religion as long as men's minds were attuned to the supernatural. It gave an "explanation" of extraordinary occurrences while it provided techniques for utilizing supernatural forces to secure advantages and to protect the members of the community against them when they were adverse.

The growth of natural science brought extraordinary things into line with events for which there is a "natural" explanation. At the same time, the development of positive social interests crowded heaven—and its opposite, hell—into the background. The function and offices of churches became more and more specialized; concerns and values that had been regarded, in an earlier contrast, as profane and secular grew in bulk and in importance. At the same time, the notion that basic and ultimate spiritual and ideal values are associated with the supernatural has persisted as a kind of vague background and aura. A kind of polite deference to the notion remains along with a concrete transfer of interest. The general mind is thus left in a confused and divided state. The movement that has been going on for the last few centuries will continue to breed doubleness of mind until religious meanings and values are definitely integrated into normal social relations.

The issue may be more definitely stated. The extreme position on one side is that apart from relation to the supernatural, man is morally on a level with the brutes. The other position is that all significant ends and all securities for stability and peace have grown up in the matrix of human relations, and that the values given a supernatural locus are in fact products of an idealizing imagination that has laid hold of natural goods. There ensues a second contrast. On the one hand, it is held that relation to the supernatural is the only finally dependable source of motive power; that directly and indirectly it has animated every serious effort for the guidance and rectification of man's life on earth. The other position is that goods actually experienced in the concrete relations of family, neighborhood, citizenship, pursuit of art and science, are what men actually depend upon for guidance and support, and that their reference to a supernatural and other-worldly locus has obscured their real nature and has weakened their force.

The contrasts outlined define the religious problem of the present and the future. What would be the consequences upon the values of human association if intrinsic and immanent satisfactions and opportunities were clearly held to and cultivated with the ardor and the devotion that have at times marked historic religions? The contention of an increasing number of persons is that depreciation of natural social values has resulted, both in principle and in actual fact, from reference of their origin and significance to supernatural sources. Natural relations, of husband and wife, of parent and child, friend and friend, neighbor and neighbor, of fellow workers in industry, science, and art, are neglected, passed over, not developed for all that is in them. They are, moreover, not merely depreciated. They have been regarded as dangerous rivals of higher values; as offering temptations to be resisted; as usurpations by flesh of the authority of the spirit; as revolts of the human against the divine.

The doctrine of original sin and total depravity, of the corruption of nature, external and internal, is not especially current in liberal religious circles at present. Rather, there prevails the idea that there are two separate systems of values—an idea similar to that referred to in the previous chapter about a revelation of two kinds of truth. The values found in natural and supernatural relationships are now, in liberal circles, said to be complementary, just as the truths of revelation and of science are the two sides, mutually sustaining, of the same ultimate truth.

I cannot but think that this position represents a great advance upon the traditional one. While it is open logically to the objections that hold against the idea of the dual revelation of truth, practically it indicates a development of a humane point of view. But if it be once admitted that human relations are charged with values that are religious in function, why not rest the case upon what is verifiable and concentrate thought and energy upon its full realization?

History seems to exhibit three stages of growth. In the first stage, human relationships were thought to be so infected with the evils of corrupt human nature as to require redemption from external and supernatural sources. In the next stage, what is significant in these relations is found to be akin to values esteemed distinctively religious. This is the point now reached by liberal theologians. The third stage would realize that in fact the values prized in those religions that have ideal elements are idealizations of things characteristic of natural association, which have then been projected into a supernatural realm for safe-keeping and sanction. Note the rôle of such terms as Father, Son, Bride,

Fellowship and Communion in the vocabulary of Christianity, and note also the tendency, even if a somewhat inchoate one, of terms that express the more intimate phases of association to displace those of legal, political origin: King, Judge, and Lord of Hosts.

Unless there is a movement into what I have called the third stage, fundamental dualism and a division in life continue. The idea of a double and parallel manifestation of the divine, in which the latter has superior status and authority, brings about a condition of unstable equilibrium. It operates to distract energy, through dividing the objects to which it is directed. It also imperatively raises the question as to why having gone far in recognition of religious values in normal community life, we should not go further. The values of natural human intercourse and mutual dependence are open and public, capable of verification by the methods through which all natural facts are established. By means of the same experimental method, they are capable of expansion. Why not concentrate upon nurturing and extending them? Unless we take this step, the idea of two realms of spiritual values is only a softened version of the old dualism between the secular and the spiritual, the profane and the religious.

The condition of unstable equilibrium is indeed so evident to the thoughtful mind that there are attempts just now to revert to the earlier stage of belief. It is not difficult to make a severe indictment of existing social relations. It is enough to point to the war, jealousy, and fear that dominate the relations of national states to one another; to the growing demoralization of the older ties of domestic life; to the staggering evidence of corruption and futility in politics, and to the egoism, brutality, and oppression that characterize economic activities. By piling up material of this sort, one may, if one chooses, arrive at the triumphant conclusion that social relations are so debased that the only recourse is to supernatural aid. The general disorder of the Great War and succeeding decades has led to a revival of the theology of corruption, sin, and need for supernatural redemption.

The conclusion does not follow, however, from the data. It ignores, in the first place, that all the positive values which are prized, and in aid of which supernatural power is appealed to, have, after all, emerged from the very scene of human associations of which it is possible to paint so black a picture. Something in the facts has been left out of the picture. I shall not bring forward again at this place what was earlier said as to the effect upon actual conditions of diversion of the thought and action of those who are peculiarly sensitive to ideal considerations into supernatural channels. I shall raise a more directly practical issue. Society is convicted of being "immoral" by evoking all the evils of institutions as they now exist, and the unexpressed premise is that the institutions as they exist are normal expressions of social relations in their own nature.

Were this premise stated, the enormous gap between it and the conclusion set forth would be apparent. The problem of the relation between social relations and institutions that are dominant at a particular time is the most intricate problem presented to social inquiry. The idea that the latter are a direct reflex of the former ignores the multiplicity of factors that historically have entered into the shaping of institutions. Historically speaking, many of these factors are accidental with respect to the institutional form that has been given to social relations. One of my favorite quotations is a statement of Clarence Ayers that "our industrial revolution began, as some historians say, with half a dozen technical improvements in the textile industry; and it took us a century to realize that anything of moment had happened to us, beyond the obvious improvement of spinning and weaving." This statement must serve in lieu of long argument to suggest what I mean by the "accidental" relation of institutional developments to the primary facts of human association. The relation is accidental because institutional consequences that have resulted were not foreseen or intended. To say this, is to say that social intelligence in the sense in which there is intelligence about physical relations is in so far nonexistent.

Here is the negative fact that renders argument for the necessity of supernatural intervention to effect significant betterment only just another instance of the old, old inference to the supernatural from the basis of ignorance. We lack, for example, knowledge of the relation of life to inanimate matter. Therefore supernatural intervention is assumed to have effected the transition from brute to man. We do not know the relation of the organism—the brain and nervous system—to the occurrence of thought. Therefore, it is argued, there is a supernatural link. We do not know the relation of causes to results in social matters, and consequently we lack means of control. Therefore, it is inferred, we must resort to supernatural control. Of course, I make no claim to knowing how far intelligence may and will develop in respect to social relations. But one thing I think I do know. The needed understanding will not develop unless we strive for it. The assumption that only supernatural agencies can give control is a sure method of retarding this effort. It is as sure to be a hindering force now with respect to social intelligence, as the similar appeal was earlier an obstruction in the development of physical knowledge.

Even immediately, without awaiting the development of greater intelligence in relation to social affairs, a great difference would be made by use of natural means and methods. It is even now possible to examine complex social phenomena sufficiently to put the finger on things that are wrong. It is possible to trace to some extent these evils to their causes, and to causes that are something very different from abstract moral forces. It is possible to work out and work upon remedies for some of the sore spots. The outcome will not be a gospel of salvation but it will be in line with that pursued, for example, in matters of disease and health. The method if used would not only accomplish something toward social health but it would accomplish a greater thing; it would forward the development of social intelligence so that it could act with greater hardihood and on a larger scale.

Vested interests, interests vested with power, are powerfully on the side of the *status quo*, and therefore they are especially powerful in hindering the growth and application of the method of natural intelligence. Just because these interests are so powerful, it is the more necessary to fight for recognition of the method of intelligence in action. But one of the greatest obstacles in conducting this combat is the tendency to dispose of social evils in terms of general moral causes. The sinfulness of man, the corruption of his heart, his self-love and love of power, when referred to as causes are precisely of the same nature as was the appeal to abstract powers (which in fact only reduplicated under a general name a multitude of particular effects) that once prevailed in physical "science," and that operated as a chief obstacle to the generation and growth of the latter. Demons were once appealed to in order to explain bodily disease and no such thing as a strictly natural death was supposed to happen. The importation of general moral causes to explain present *social* phenomena is on the same intellectual level. Reinforced by the prestige of traditional religions, and backed by the emotional force of beliefs in the supernatural, it stifles the growth of that social intelligence by means of which direction of social change could be taken out of the region of accident, as accident has been defined. Accident in this broad sense and the idea of the supernatural are twins. Interest in the supernatural therefore reinforces other vested interests to prolong the social reign of accident.

There is a strong reaction in some religious circles today against the idea of mere individual salvation of individual souls. There is also a reaction in politics and economics against the idea of *laissez faire*. Both of these movements reflect a common tendency. Both of them are signs of the growing awareness of the emptiness of individuality in isolation. But the fundamental root of the *laissez faire* idea is denial (more often implicit than express) of the possibility of radical intervention of intelligence in the conduct of human life. Now appeal for supernatural intervention in improvement of social matters is also the expression of a deep-seated *laissez-faireism*; it is the acknowledgment of the desperate situation into which we are driven by the idea of the irrelevance and futility of human intervention in social events and interests. Those contemporary theologians who are interested in social change and who at the same time depreciate human intelligence and effort in behalf of the supernatural, are riding two horses that are going in opposite directions. The old-fashioned ideas of doing something to make the will of God prevail in the world, and of assuming the responsibility of doing the job ourselves, have more to be said for them, logically and practically.

The emphasis that has been put upon intelligence as a method should not mislead anyone. Intelligence, as distinct from the older conception of reason, is inherently involved in action. Moreover, there is no opposition between it and emotion. There is such a thing as passionate intelligence, as ardor in behalf of light shining into the murky places of social existence, and as zeal for its refreshing and purifying effect. The whole story of man shows that there are no objects that may not deeply stir engrossing emotion. One of the few experiments in the attachment of emotion to ends that mankind has not tried is that of devotion, so intense as to be religious, to intelligence as a force in social action.

But this is only part of the scene. No matter how much evidence may be piled up against social institutions as they exist, affection and passionate desire for justice and security are realities in human nature. So are the emotions that arise from living in conditions of inequity, oppression, and insecurity. Combination of the two kinds of emotion has more than once produced those changes that go by the name of revolution. To say that emotions which are not fused with intelligence are blind is tautology. Intense emotion may utter itself in action that destroys institutions. But the only assurance of birth of better ones is the marriage of emotion with intelligence.

Criticism of the commitment of religion to the supernatural is thus positive in import. All modes of human association are "affected with a public interest," and full realization of this interest is equivalent to a sense of a significance that is religious in its function. The objection to supernaturalism is that it stands in the way of an effective realization of the sweep and depth of the implications of natural human relations. It stands in the way of using the means that are in our power to make radical changes in these relations. It is certainly true that great material changes might be made with no corresponding improvement of a spiritual or ideal nature. But development in the latter direction cannot be introduced from without; it cannot be brought about by dressing up material and economic changes with decorations derived from the supernatural. It can come only from more intense realization of values that inhere in the actual connections of human beings with one another. The attempt to segregate the implicit public interest and social value of all institutions and social arrangements in a particular organization is a fatal diversion.

Were men and women actuated throughout the length and breadth of human relations with the faith and ardor that have at times marked historic religions the consequences would be incalculable. To achieve this faith and *élan* is no easy task. But religions have attempted something similar, directed moreover toward a less promising object—the supernatural. It does not become those who hold that faith may move mountains to deny in advance the possibility of its manifestation on the basis of verifiable realities. There already exists, though in a rudimentary form, the capacity to relate social conditions and events to their causes, and the ability will grow with exercise. There is the technical skill with which to initiate a campaign for social health and sanity analogous to that made in behalf of physical public health. Human beings have impulses toward affection, compassion and justice, equality and freedom. It remains to weld all these things together. It is of no use merely to assert that the intrenched foes of class interest and power in high places are hostile to the realization of such a union. As I have already said, if this enemy did not exist, there would be little sense in urging *any* policy of change. The point to be grasped is that, unless one gives up the whole struggle as hopeless, one has to choose between alternatives. One alternative is dependence upon the supernatural; the other, the use of natural agencies.

There is then no sense, logical or practical, in pointing out the difficulties that stand in the way of the latter course, until the question of the alternative is faced. If it is faced, it will also be realized that one factor in the choice is dependence upon enlisting only those committed to the supernatural and alliance with all men and women who feel the stir of social emotion, including the large number of those who, consciously or unconsciously, have turned their backs upon the supernatural. Those who face the alternatives will also have to choose between a continued and even more systematic *laissez faire* depreciation of intelligence and the resources of natural knowledge and understanding, and conscious and organized effort to turn the use of these means from narrow ends, personal and class, to larger human purposes. They will have to ask, as far as they nominally believe in the need for radical social change, whether what they accomplish when they point with one hand to the seriousness of present evils is not undone when the other hand points away from man and nature for their remedy.

The transfer of idealizing imagination, thought and emotion to natural human relations would not signify the destruction of churches that now exist. It would rather offer the means for a recovery of vitality. The fund of human values that are prized and that need to be cherished, values that are satisfied and rectified by *all* human concerns and arrangements, could be celebrated and reinforced, in different ways and with differing symbols, by the churches. In that way the churches would indeed become catholic. The demand that churches show a more active interest in social affairs, that they take a definite stand upon such questions as war, economic injustice, political corruption, that they stimulate action for a divine kingdom on earth, is one of the signs of the times. But as long as social values are related to a supernatural for which the churches stand in some peculiar way, there is an inherent inconsistency between the demand and efforts to execute it. On the one hand, it is urged that the churches are going outside their special province when they involve themselves in economic and political issues. On the other hand, the very fact that they claim if not a monopoly of supreme values and motivating forces, yet a unique relation

to them, makes it impossible for the churches to participate
in promotion of social ends on a natural and equal human
basis. The surrender of claims to an exclusive and authoritative position is a *sine qua non* for doing away with the di-
lemma in which churches now find themselves in respect to
their sphere of social action.

At the outset, I referred to an outstanding historic fact.
The coincidence of the realm of social interests and activities with a tribal or civic community has vanished. Secular interests and activities have grown up outside of organized religions and are independent of their authority. The
hold of these interests upon the thoughts and desires of
men has crowded the social importance of organized religions into a corner and the area of this corner is decreasing.
This change either marks a terrible decline in everything
that can justly be termed religious in value, in traditional
religions, or it provides the opportunity for expansion of
these qualities on a new basis and with a new outlook. It is
impossible to ignore the fact that historic Christianity has
been committed to a separation of sheep and goats; the
saved and the lost; the elect and the mass. Spiritual aristoc-
racy as well as *laissez faire* with respect to natural and human intervention, is deeply embedded in its traditions. Lip
service—often more than lip service—has been given to the
idea of the common brotherhood of all men. But those
outside the fold of the church and those who do not rely
upon belief in the supernatural have been regarded as only
potential brothers, still requiring adoption into the family. I
cannot understand how any realization of the democratic
ideal as a vital moral and spiritual ideal in human affairs is

possible without surrender of the conception of the basic division to which supernatural Christianity is committed. Whether or no we are, save in some metaphorical sense, all brothers, we are at least all in the same boat traversing the same turbulent ocean. The potential religious significance of this fact is infinite.

In the opening chapter I made a distinction between religion and the religious. I pointed out that religion—or religions—is charged with beliefs, practices and modes of organization that have accrued to and been loaded upon the religious element in experience by the state of culture in which religions have developed. I urged that conditions are now ripe for emancipation of the religious quality from accretions that have grown up about it and that limit the credibility and the influence of religion. In the second chapter, I developed this idea with respect to the faith in ideals that is immanent in the religious value of experience, and asserted that the power of this faith would be enhanced were belief freed from the conception that the significance and validity of the ideal are bound up with intellectual assent to the proposition that the ideal is already embodied in some supernatural or metaphysical sense in the very framework of existence.

The matter touched upon in the present chapter includes within itself all that has been previously set forth. It does so upon both its negative and positive sides. The community of causes and consequences in which we, together with those not born, are enmeshed is the widest and deepest symbol of the mysterious totality of being the imagination calls the universe. It is the embodiment for sense and thought of that encompassing scope of existence the intellect cannot grasp. It is the matrix within which our ideal aspirations are born and bred. It is the source of the values that the moral imagination projects as directive criteria and as shaping purposes. The continuing life of this comprehensive community of beings includes all the significant achievement of men in science and art and all the kindly offices of intercourse and communication. It holds within its content all the material that gives verifiable intellectual support to our ideal faiths. A "creed" founded on this material will change and grow, but it cannot be shaken. What it surrenders it gives up gladly because of new light and not as a reluctant concession. What it adds, it adds because new knowledge gives further insight into the conditions that bear upon the formation and execution of our life purposes. A one-sided psychology, a reflex of eighteenth-century "individualism," treated knowledge as an accomplishment of a lonely mind. We should now be aware that it is a product of the cooperative and communicative operations of human beings living together. Its communal origin is an indication of its rightful communal use. The unification of what is known at any given time, not upon an impossible eternal and abstract basis but upon that of its bearing upon the unification of human desire and purpose, furnishes a sufficient creed for human acceptance, one that would provide a religious release and reinforcement of knowledge.

"Agnosticism" is a shadow cast by the eclipse of the supernatural. Of course, acknowledgment that we do not know what we do not know is a necessity of all intellectual integrity. But generalized agnosticism is only a halfway elimination of the supernatural. Its meaning departs when the intellectual outlook is directed wholly to the natural world. When it is so directed, there are plenty of particular matters regarding which we must say we do not know; we only inquire and form hypotheses which future inquiry will confirm or reject. But such doubts are an incident of faith in the method of intelligence. They are signs of faith, not of a pale and impotent skepticism. We doubt in order that we may find out, not because some inaccessible supernatural lurks behind whatever *we* can know. The substantial background of practical faith in ideal ends is positive and outreaching.

The considerations put forward in the present chapter may be summed up in what they imply. The ideal ends to which we attach our faith are not shadowy and wavering. They assume concrete form in our understanding of our relations to one another and the values contained in these relations. We who now live are parts of a humanity that extends into the remote past, a humanity that has interacted with nature. The things in civilization we most prize are not of ourselves. They exist by grace of the doings and sufferings of the continuous human community in which we are a link. Ours is the responsibility of conserving, transmitting, rectifying and expanding the heritage of values we have received that those who come after us may receive it more solid and secure, more widely accessible and more generously shared than we have received it. Here are all the elements for a religious faith that shall not be confined to sect, class, or race. Such a faith has always been implicitly the common faith of mankind. It remains to make it explicit and militant.

Natural

Spiritual —

all purpose
loving

eternal

Religious Isolation
but modern
spirituality
is isolating

american
growing   no religious
with ident.fication

writer
Blake → Nat'l
          in[ ]uty
Dohnn?
E. Burke –
Santayana
Emerson
Wadworth

K. Burke
Nabokov
Cultural revolution

Natural piety = sublime - solitude
    identify twg sublime

Filial piety - duties
    Burke's   connection,
        contemplated   identify from relationship

Religious piety -
    Ritual
    control passions
    identify two
        connection to God
        & other worshippers
    worship not
            belief
    O'Connor